BUILDING A
WELLNESS
BUSINESS
THAT LASTS

BUILDING A
WELLNESS
BUSINESS
THAT LASTS

HOW TO MAKE A GREAT LIVING
DOING WHAT YOU LOVE

RICK STOLLMEYER

WILEY

Library of Congress Cataloging-in-Publication Data:

Names: Stollmeyer, Rick, author.
Title: Building a wellness business that lasts : how to make a great living doing what you love / Rick Stollmeyer.
Description: Hoboken, New Jersey : John Wiley & Sons, Inc., [2021] | Includes bibliographical references and index.
Identifiers: LCCN 2020039056 (print) | LCCN 2020039057 (ebook) | ISBN 9781119679066 (cloth) | ISBN 9781119679158 (adobe pdf) | ISBN 9781119679141 (epub)
Subjects: LCSH: Alternative medicine specialists. | Mind and body therapies. | New business enterprises. | Business planning. | Entrepreneurship.
Classification: LCC R733 .S761215 2021 (print) | LCC R733 (ebook) | DDC 610—dc23
LC record available at https://lccn.loc.gov/2020039056
LC ebook record available at https://lccn.loc.gov/2020039057

Cover Design: Wiley
Cover Image: © MindBody logo (enso) © MINDBODY, Inc.

10 9 8 7 6 5 4 3 2 1

For the people who risk it all to help others live healthier, happier lives and the people who love them.

Contents

INTRODUCTION

This Book Is for the Wellness Community

There is a powerful movement happening, already in full swing pre-COVID-19 and accelerated by the pandemic. In nearly every country on earth, billions of people are prioritizing their health and happiness like never before. They are recognizing that their best life is not found through the endless accumulation of money and things, but rather through meaningful relationships, memorable experiences, a sense of purpose, and optimal health.

People are waking up to the truth that sustained happiness requires a definition of health that goes far beyond the expectations of prior generations. Rather than simply pursuing a body and mind free from disease, they are pursuing a vision of health that optimizes every facet of their lives, addresses their whole person, and increases their resilience to disease. People are looking for health that not only gives more years in their lives, but also more life in their years.

This new definition of health is called *wellness*, and chances are, you picked up this book because you already sense these trends. You have incorporated healthier eating, exercise, and multiple other wellness practices into your life, and you have a newfound sense of purpose. You have become a wellness evangelist with those you are closest to, and now you want to share your passion with others.

For all who feel the calling of life as a wellness professional, this book is for you.

You may already be a wellness professional. You've been teaching classes, training people, and delivering life-changing experiences for years. COVID-19 disrupted your life in 2020, and now you dream of leveraging new technologies to achieve independence, designing your own experiences, setting your own schedule, and being your own boss.

For all who seek self-employment in the wellness industry, this book is for you.

Or you may be dreaming of an even greater leap—creating your own neighborhood wellness business or launching a digital wellness brand. You've studied the experiences delivered by others and you know you can do better. You noticed the many *For Lease* signs in your neighborhood and have been thinking about business names, studio layouts, and experience delivery. You may be sharing this vision with potential partners and two or three of you are considering taking the leap together.

For all who audaciously dream of launching a wellness business that catches the next wave of the wellness revolution by employing others and serving thousands, this book is for you.

Or you may have already taken that leap and launched your wellness business and difficult realities have set in. COVID-19 hit your business hard, depleted your savings, and left you indebted. That economic catastrophe hit on top of your usual daily challenges of leaky roofs; toilets that don't flush; troublesome landlords; and the neighbor who makes too much noise, emits strange smells every afternoon, or complains about you doing the same.

Then there's your team. The ones you love but who can't seem to show up on time. The ones your clients love but who create drama behind the scenes. Or the perfect employee who just told you she has fallen in love and is moving out of state—next week.

All of these normal daily challenges sit on top of a simple and terrifying reality: without a continuous flow of new and returning clients, your business won't last, and the dream you poured your heart and soul into will morph into a nightmare that may take every last penny you have.

For all who are bravely facing the challenges of creating a thriving wellness business in a post-COVID world, this book is for you.

Or your wellness business may be stable but you're wondering, "What's next?" You successfully weathered the COVID-19 storm and surmounted numerous other challenges. You've received government funding and are back to taking home a comfortable income, your debt is manageable, your team is (mostly) reliable, and your clients are (mostly) happy. But the challenge of the shut down and the daily grind is taking its toll. Your days have begun to feel repetitive and you're secretly growing tired of it.

What began as your ultimate creative expression of self has turned into a really demanding job. You're working way too many hours and there is a tiny voice inside saying, "It's time to change it up or move on." Maybe your creative spirit has been captured by a fresh new idea. Or maybe you just need an extended vacation.

For all who have built a thriving wellness business and are now standing at a crossroads, this book is for you.

Regardless of which of these descriptions best reflects your reality, please know that you are not alone. Thousands of brave souls have walked the path you are on now, and many principles they have learned are timeless and universal. And many new principles are coming into existence post COVID-19. You will learn these principles in a simple and clear way in the chapters ahead.

The COVID-19 Thunderbolt

In the first half of 2020, COVID-19 hit the wellness industry like a bolt of lightning—sudden, unexpected, and devastating in its effect.

Simultaneously across more than ninety countries, the global wellness industry shut down. I know because the company I co-founded with Blake Beltram, Mindbody, handles the client bookings for much of the industry. More than 90 percent of the businesses on our platform were forced to shut their doors, either in response to government mandate or falling consumer demand, and more than 80 percent of total business activity disappeared—and it stayed that way for months.

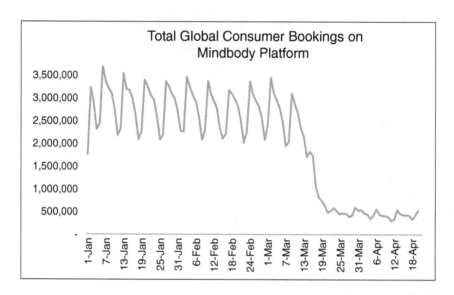

In the midst of the dual public health and economic crisis presented by COVID-19, the seeds of our industry's future were being sown. Within days of the global collapse of our industry that began on March 11, thousands of wellness business owners were implementing virtual delivery of their services. Staying connected to their clientele and delivering wellness classes and appointments via Zoom, Instagram, WhatsApp, and other virtual techniques had become mission critical.

At Mindbody, our own software development team went into overdrive to accelerate the delivery of an integrated Virtual Wellness Platform, enabling wellness business owners of any size to upload both prerecorded classes and streaming video, restricting access of that content to paying clients only, and selling hybrid face-to-face and virtual memberships. And the people came.

In the weeks following the official declaration of the COVID-19 pandemic, we saw exponential growth of virtual wellness delivery as people sheltering at home logged into classes and appointments from their laptops, phones, and tablets. In the months that followed, as communities around the world gradually reopened and brick-and-mortar studios were once again allowed to welcome paying customers into their places of business, we saw that virtual delivery had become an important and enduring component of wellness—in addition to the brick-and-mortar offline experiences.

In short, the sudden bolt of COVID-19 lightning that so dramatically disrupted our industry in 2020 has become a spark that ignited yet another wave of wellness industry growth and innovation. This wave promises to be even larger and more exciting than the last.

My Journey to the Wellness Industry

This book is not about Mindbody or me, but in case you are wondering where the knowledge and opinions in the pages that follow come from, here's the short story:

I was raised in a small-business family. My grandfather, parents, and three of my four brothers were all small-business owners. I began working at Stollmeyer Lighting—our family's retail lighting store—when I was 10 years old. My dad and older brothers taught me to assemble and display light fixtures, sweep floors, and clean. Within a few years I was on the showroom floor selling light fixtures and in the back office learning how to keep the books and understand financial statements.

My family was proud of my entrepreneurial parents. My mom and dad were different from other people. They were independent in their thinking and daring in their pursuit of the American Dream. People in the community respected and looked up to them. My parents didn't have jobs; they created them.

But there was another side to this story.

What others outside the family rarely saw were the hard realities of making a living with a small business. Decorative lighting sales rode the crests and troughs of the economy. Stollmeyer Lighting flourished when homes were being built or remodeled. But when the inevitable recessions came—and there were several in the 1970s, 1980s, and 1990s—sales would plummet and the store would morph from a nicely profitable family business into a cash-burning machine, quickly eating into my parents' nest egg.

One of those recessions hit as I was entering high school in the early 1980s. Our comfortable upper-middle-class household was soon pushed into financial crisis. I was a strong student and could see the seriousness in my parents' eyes as they urged me to excel in school, go to college, and "get credentials" so that I might have a more financially secure future than they did. They vowed to pay for any university I could get into and encouraged me to dream big. I internalized their message and knew deep down that I would never ask them for a penny.

Instead, I threw myself into school and aimed for straight A's so that I might earn a scholarship to a top university. Near the end of my junior year, a classmate told me about the Service Academies—the U.S. Naval Academy in Annapolis, Maryland; the U.S. Military Academy in West Point, New York; the U.S. Air Force Academy in Colorado Springs, Colorado; and the U.S. Coast Guard Academy in New London, Connecticut. These are all top-rated universities and they pay their students to attend, including free room and board. Successful graduates not only receive a bachelor's degree but are guaranteed a job as commissioned officers in their respective service branches. I liked the sound of that.

Three weeks after throwing my high school graduation cap into the air, I reported to the U.S. Naval Academy. I knew very little about the Navy except that they had cool-looking ships, awesome jets, and the best-looking uniforms. I figured my experience at Annapolis would be like Harvard with some Navy training thrown in. Boy was I wrong.

By accepting an appointment to Annapolis, I had committed myself to one of the most physically, emotionally, and academically challenging programs in the world. After the first week, we were given a brief break and allowed to call our parents. When I heard my mom's voice, I burst into tears. I could scarcely get any words out. She and my dad must have thought they were torturing me, but I was just exhausted and homesick. We weren't tortured, but we were hazed. The truth is I really hated the place and the place didn't think much of me. But I was seriously stubborn. I wanted the free education and I wanted to be a naval officer. They could kick me out, but I sure as hell wasn't going to quit.

Although several upperclassmen tried to drive me out, they didn't succeed. In the end, with the emotional support of my parents, the help of my classmates, and a few blessed doses of good luck, I graduated, received my commission as an ensign in the Navy, and was selected for the nuclear submarine program.

I served aboard the USS *Chicago* (SSN-721), a fast attack submarine doing important missions in the Western Pacific. This was in the final years of the Cold War with the Soviet Union and our ship participated in multiple missions designed to prevent a hot war from breaking out. Most of these I can never talk about, but I can say that we were fortunate to never go into battle, damage the ship, or lose a shipmate. But the real specter of those possibilities hung over us constantly. It was dangerous work and unbelievably intense. A nuclear submarine is one of the most complex machines ever created, and keeping it running safely is a constant battle against the elements. A submarine crew works 24/7 and sleep quickly becomes the most precious commodity.

When I left the Navy at age 28, I was a profoundly stronger person than the scared kid who had broken down in tears at the sound of his mother's voice a decade earlier. Those were hard years, but they were purpose-driven and they introduced me to some of the best people I have ever known. Most important, the Navy showed me about the hidden strength inside each of us, taught me humility, and gave me a global perspective. Staring into the face of war for ten years, I became deeply committed to peace.

In my first six years after the Navy I held six different engineering management jobs in four different companies. None of those roles inspired me and I began to feel that I must not be cut out for business. What I was really feeling were my family's entrepreneurial roots tugging at me. In 2000, I left corporate America behind to co-found Mindbody with my high school buddy Blake Beltram and ran that business as president or CEO for nearly twenty years.

Blake was also raised in a small-business family, and we shared a deep empathy for the scrappy grass-roots entrepreneurs who were opening neighborhood boutique studios in Los Angeles, San Francisco, and New York. These people were leading a boutique fitness movement that we would later identify as the *Second Wave of Wellness* (see Chapter 3, "The Generational Lens"), and they included two amazingly powerful women who would play pivotal roles in our future. The first was Mari Winsor, the "Pilates Teacher to the Stars" who had engaged Blake to build a PC software solution that could manage and link her hugely successful Beverly Hills and West Hollywood studios. The second was Blake's future wife, Cynthia Graham, a Black entrepreneur and wellness innovator who together with her sister Karyn opened RPM Studios in 1998, one of the first Spinning® studios in the San Fernando Valley.

Mindbody's first products were PC software solutions designed to help wellness business owners simplify their operations, boost their revenues, and stay connected to their clients. But we had much bigger dreams. We envisioned a platform that could help drive millions more people to those studios and thereby connect the world to wellness. That intention would later be captured in Mindbody's Purpose Statement:

To Help People Lead Healthier, Happier Lives by Connecting the World to Wellness

Achieving our vision would prove to be much harder than we ever imagined. But thanks to the good faith of hundreds of early adopter customers, the help of multiple mentors and investors, and the talented efforts of thousands of team members, our vision has been realized.

Mindbody now helps tens of millions of consumers engage with tens of thousands of wellness businesses worldwide. Our platform manages both retail brick-and-mortar and virtual wellness businesses, including many hybrid businesses that have sprung up since COVID-19. Our company employs more than 1,400 team members in offices on four continents, and millions of wellness experiences are managed on our platform each day.

There was much we didn't know twenty years ago about building a software business. We didn't even know how much we didn't know. But we did know the most important thing for any entrepreneur: our customers. By keeping those customers as our North Star and striving constantly to know them better, we were able to figure out the rest.

In this book you will gain a deeper understanding of the wellness industry and learn how to define your ideal customers. Armed with that insight, you will learn how to prepare yourself for success, conceive a wellness business that lasts, and launch that business successfully.

My life's journey has included many hard lessons, most learned with the help of friends, customers, and mentors and several with accompanying doses of pain along the way. My ultimate purpose in writing this book is to pay that forward, passing along as many hard-earned lessons as possible.

Whether your dream is to be an independent wellness practitioner, small business owner, or creator of the next global brand, I hope this book inspires you, helps you to better target and serve your customers profitably, and saves you from learning some lessons the hard way.

PART I

Understand the Wellness Industry

1 | Making a Living in Wellness

Building a successful and sustainable wellness business is far from easy. This industry, which began in earnest in the late 1970s, has been subject to changing consumer tastes, rapidly evolving technologies, and unpredictable disruptions ever since. The fitness class or wellness service that is hot today could be old news in a few years, and every once in a while an unexpected disaster like 9/11, a sharp economic downturn, or COVID-19 can upend your carefully laid plans.

Many prospective wellness entrepreneurs don't want to hear that, particularly yoga and Pilates teachers, and practitioners of ancient arts such as Ayurveda and traditional Chinese medicine. Yes, these practices are centuries old and proven to work. But, as a business owner, your principal challenge is not whether your modality works. Your principal challenge is how to deliver experiences around that modality that tomorrow's consumers will pay for so that you can earn a sustainable profit. This is the essential ingredient of a successful wellness business.

As we will lay out in the next chapter, the modern wellness movement has occurred in three distinct waves, each driven by the arrival of a new generation of adults coupled with key advancements of technology. Now in the 2020s, we are surely on the cusp of yet another wave, the onset of which has been accelerated by COVID-19. In the decade to come, we can be certain that hundreds of millions more people will make wellness a top priority in their lives. What we cannot be certain of is which wellness practices and forms of delivery those people will favor. But we can make educated guesses both by understanding the societal forces that have shaped the modern wellness movement and by being astute observers of the trends happening around us.

Most important, we can commit ourselves to business plans that are agile and hedged against future disruptions and that are capable of absorbing economic shocks and rapidly adapting to match changing technologies and consumer tastes.

Therefore, to successfully create wellness businesses that last, we must embrace a paradox. We must be disciplined enough to prepare ourselves and create well-thought-out plans, committed enough to see our plans to fruition, and nimble enough to change course when our concepts don't work or the tide turns against us. This means staying grounded in the timeless principles of the wellness experience—movement, nutrition, mindfulness, and social connection—while staying flexible in how best to deliver these outcomes to our clients.

The best way to do that is to closely watch and experience other wellness businesses around you. As you do this you will observe what they are doing well and what they are not. You will take careful note of why the most effective wellness businesses are successful and why the least effective are not. Both examples are necessary and important. In fact, the bad examples may teach you even more than the good ones.

If you are a veteran business owner whose numbers have stagnated or started to fall, you may identify with this statement:

That new flavor of the month wellness business that just popped up and is stealing all my clients. Meanwhile, my business steeped in time-honored tradition is suffering..

If this describes how you are feeling, I first want to acknowledge your pain. You worked so hard to learn your craft and build your business. You have served so many people and enhanced so many lives. And now it feels like the upstart is taking them from you. That hurts.

Okay, now I want you to set that baggage down and consider what Khalil Gibran said more than 100 years ago in his poem *On Children*:

You may strive to be like them,
but seek not to make them like you.
For life goes not backward nor tarries with yesterday.

As entrepreneurs, the businesses we create feel like our children. And as with actual children, their growth is marked by repeated opportunities to choose between bravely moving toward their future or staying stuck in the past. In business as in life, one is either growing or dying.

And what is true for the parent is also true for the entrepreneur. Choosing to raise a child or start and run a business is a Hero's Journey.

The Hero's Journey

In his landmark book *The Hero with a Thousand Faces*, Joseph Campbell defined an archetypal human journey found in every culture, mythology, and faith tradition. This "Hero's Journey" is captured today in the movies we love, from the *Wizard of Oz* and *Casablanca,* to *The Graduate* and *Star Wars*, to *Forrest Gump, Guardians of the Galaxy,* and *Apollo 13.*

Joseph Campbell summarized this Journey as follows:

A hero ventures forth from the world of common day into a region of supernatural wonder:
fabulous forces are there encountered and a decisive victory is won:
the hero comes back from this mysterious adventure with the power to bestow boons on his fellow man

Let's break this down.

A hero ventures forth from the world of common day . . .

The United States is the most entrepreneurial nation on earth and the birth-place of the modern wellness movement, yet even in the United States less than 6 percent of U.S. adults earn a living owning any business and less than 0.5 percent are employed in the wellness industry.

In short, wellness professionals and entrepreneurs are a rare breed. They are heroes who have made a conscious decision to leave the comfort of the world most people consider normal. They have chosen to leave the comfort and safety of a conventional job, in many cases taking dramatic cuts in pay and benefits and in other cases leaving behind regular pay and benefits altogether. If you choose to strike out on your own as an independent contractor or small business owner, you also leave behind paid vacations, 40-hour workweeks, and most government labor law protections.

When you launch your own wellness business, in the early stages, you will likely find yourself working 60–80 hours per week and drawing little or no cash from your business. And unless you have a wealthy partner or benefactor, you will most likely find yourself drawing from personal savings, running up credit cards, and borrowing from friends and family to ensure that your own employees and landlord get paid.

And you will be doing all of this to help other people live healthier, happier lives. That makes you a hero in my book. In every sense of the word.

. . . into a region of supernatural wonder . . .

To start a wellness business is to enter into the world of the marketplace, a mysterious land where unseen forces and unpredictable outcomes rule the day. When you open your doors, you will learn things about your community you never knew. You will become one of a small band of people in your community who have each taken similarly daring leaps. And you will find yourself searching online or looking at your neighborhood with new eyes, asking the ultimate question:

Thousands of people search for what I do every day. Why aren't more of them coming to me?

. . . fabulous forces are there encountered . . .

The moment you begin offering wellness experiences, your services will not just be competing with other classes and appointments offered in your neighborhood. They will also be pitted against the nearly infinite array of choices we all have to fill our time. The fact is, fewer than one in five people are actively engaged in any form of organized wellness. For multiple reasons, many industry experts and I believe this level of engagement and the overall wellness industry will grow rapidly in the decade ahead, but as a wellness entrepreneur your biggest competition isn't the studio, gym, or spa down the street. It's not even Peloton® or the various on-demand or streaming classes now readily available online. Your greatest competition as a wellness entrepreneur is the couch and the latest video game or series on Amazon Prime.

So what fabulous forces could compel someone to set down the easy distractions of modern life and replace those with a challenging new wellness habit? These forces will seem supernatural at first, but there is a formula you can follow that will take most of the mystery away. The key elements are found in Chapter 12, "Lay Your Foundation with Your Competitive Advantage," Chapter 17 – "Build Your Website and Start Guerilla Marketing", and Chapter 19 "Grow Your Clientele with Paid Marketing That Works."

. . . and a decisive victory is won . . .

In short, creating a successful wellness business that lasts is profoundly difficult. It will stretch and grow you in ways you never imagined. But when you decode the supernatural wonder and prevail against the fabulous forces, there are few victories in life so sweet. It's like summitting a high mountain, experiencing the most fabulous sex, or bringing a child into the world. Creating a wellness business that lasts is thrilling, humbling, ecstatic, and heartrending—all at the same time.

A few months after we started Mindbody, a close friend who owned her own spa treated me to a massage. I was seriously stressed and needed it badly. In the middle of the treatment, she asked me in a soft voice, "So, how does it feel to have your own business?"

I was in a deeply meditative place and took my time responding:

". . . I feel . . ."

"Truly alive," she finished knowingly.

"Exactly."

. . . the hero comes back from this mysterious adventure with the power to bestow boons on his fellow man.

Regardless of the ultimate outcome, the mysterious adventure of creating your own wellness business will give you the power to bestow boons. Even if your first business venture is not "successful," the journey will teach you valuable lessons that will inform your next venture. Even if you decide to simply go to work for someone else, your insights from that venture will make you uniquely valuable to your next employer. At Mindbody, we *love* to hire entrepreneurs. These are the people who get how hard business really is and who reflexively look for ways to add more value to the organization. That is a huge boon to anyone they choose to work for.

And if your business succeeds, you will help hundreds or even thousands of people live healthier, happier lives. You will help transform your community and inspire untold numbers of others to take similar leaps. Those are powerful boons!

The Hero's Journey was never meant to be easy. But if you have what it takes, it is the best thing you can do in your professional life. Regardless of the outcome, the journey is utterly worth it. Perhaps that's the whole point.

In the months ahead, as you embark on your own Hero's Journey, you will most likely have moments of discouragement, exasperation, and doubt. In those times, refer back to the Hero's Journey to remind yourself that this is all part of the process. You will get through this!

2

The Seven Dimensions of Wellness and Maslow's Hierarchy of Needs

The Global Wellness Institute defines *wellness* as "the active pursuit of activities, choices, and lifestyles that lead to a state of holistic health." The operative words are *active pursuit*, and the fundamental truth is that most people need a highly trained practitioner—a teacher, trainer, therapist, or coach—to materially improve their wellness. Wellness is personal. It is about people helping people, and that truth is why the wellness industry exists.

The Mindbody team has been serving the wellness industry for more than two decades and we have witnessed unprecedented growth in that time. Growing at more than twice the rate of the rest of the global economy, the combined value of the wellness industry pre-COVID-19 surpassed $4.5 *trillion* in 2019 (Global Wellness Institute Report, October 2019). To put that unfathomable number into perspective, humanity spent more on wellness products and services in 2019 than they did on eating out, and 2019 was a record year for restaurants as well.

But all of that was before COVID-19 disrupted our lives, introducing the entire world to a new fear of an unseen enemy few had ever imagined, and upending the economies of the world. That unprecedented global crisis permanently changed the world view and priorities of billions of people, accelerating many societal and technological trends already in motion before the virus hit, introducing a several new trends and interrupting multiple others. The most important question to those of us in the wellness industry is what will happen to our cause and our businesses now as the world recovers from the pandemic and adjusts to a new normal.

Will the wellness industry as we know it still exist in five years? Absolutely! In fact, we are about to experience a massive new wave of growth.

All the research the Mindbody team has done, all the data we have looked at, all of our conversations with industry thought leaders, and all of the rapid technological innovations we are participating in point to one fabulous truth. The next ten years will surely to produce more wellness industry growth than the past two decades combined—regardless of economic recession, social distancing, and virus-related fears. Thanks to COVID-19, wellness has become the largest and most important issue of our age. In the decade ahead, humanity will surely invest and participate in wellness pursuits more than ever before. COVID-19 has in fact ushered in a new wave of wellness, one that will create myriad business opportunities for innovative practitioners and entrepreneurs alike.

Here's the bad news: Many of the wellness business models that were flourishing in the years leading up to COVID-19 simply won't work anymore. The COVID-19 thunderbolt has suddenly and permanently shifted our reality, and as wellness entrepreneurs we must adapt to that new reality or our businesses will die.

To understand how to fully embrace the future, we must first travel back in time and perform a thought experiment. Close your eyes and imagine traveling back in time 100 years. You are sitting with your great-grandmother at her kitchen table. What would you ask her? Imagine asking these questions:

"Great-grandma, how do you stay physically fit?"
"What tools do you use to manage stress and maintain peace of mind?"
"How do you nurture meaningful relationships?"
"What are you doing to expand your mind?"
"What are you doing to protect the environment?"
"Do you find your work fulfilling?"
"What gives your life a sense of purpose?"

What we're talking about, of course, is wellness—in fact, the Seven Dimensions of Wellness—and I'm not sure about your great-grandmother, but I'm confident mine would have responded with something like this:

"What's the point of these questions, dear? Your great-grandfather and I are trying to put food on the table and keep a roof over our heads. We lost one son to World War I a few years ago and the other to the Spanish Flu Pandemic. Our biggest concern now is their younger brother being sent off to another war, or our daughter dying in childbirth. What gives me a sense of purpose? Keeping my family alive! Now, you look hungry. Let me get you something to eat."

The Seven Dimensions of Wellness

What we are talking about with our great-grandmother in that imaginary conversation are the dimensions of wellness, and these are the central pursuits that drive most people alive today:

Physical Well-being: Keeping our bodies healthy and working optimally for as many years as possible

Emotional Well-being: Having the capacity to cope with the stresses of life

Social Well-being: Staying connected with our community, having the ability to maintain meaningful relationships, and finding love

Intellectual Well-being: Keeping our minds sharp and continually enhancing our wisdom and knowledge of the world

Environmental Well-being: Living in clean, nontoxic surroundings and protecting our planet

Occupational Well-being: Finding work that feeds our mind, body, and soul

Spiritual Well-being: Discovering the purpose and meaning of our lives

These are the Seven Dimensions of Wellness (shown in Figure 2.1), and our questions around them confused our great-grandmother, because she did not live in a world where she could spend much time thinking about them.

Unless your great-grandmother was among society's elites, she would have been as baffled by the wellness conversation as mine. This is because for nearly all of the first 200,000 years of existence, people simply didn't have

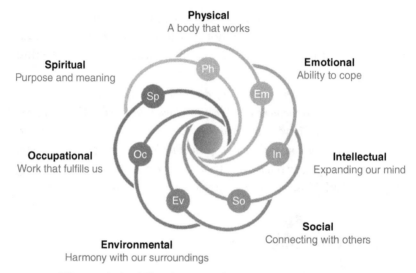

Figure 2.1   The Seven Dimensions of Wellness

the time or resources for wellness. The vast majority of them existed at the basic subsistence level, meaning their daily lives revolved around securing food, shelter, and physical safety—on staying alive and producing children.

For those whose lives could be cut short by childbirth, war, disease, or famine, the causes seemed supernatural and outside of their control. All of us alive today are the descendants of those who survived those incredibly difficult millennia, and their suffering became our strength. Our adaptive minds, our instinct to create family units, our ability to form functioning societies, and our robust immune systems are all the result of hundreds of thousands of years of human evolution.

Despite those inherent strengths, until very recently average life expectancy was only a fraction of what it is today. The average life expectancy of a Roman citizen was 25 years. One thousand years later during the Middle Ages, life expectancy had reached only 33 years. A thousand years after that—around the time we are having that imaginary conversation with our great-grandmother—average life expectancy had reached only 55 years. Through all those eons of time the highest aspiration of nearly every human being was to survive long enough to produce successful offspring.

That is why people got married so young and why the marriage contract included the phrase " 'til death do us part." People needed to start producing children as teenagers in order to have a reasonable chance of raising those kids into adulthood before they died, and death wasn't that far away.

Who had the time to think about wellness in a life like that?

To understand the relevance of this to our lives today, we need to understand Maslow's hierarchy of needs.

Maslow's Hierarchy of Needs: The Force Driving Wellness Industry Growth

In 1943, noted American psychologist and researcher Abraham Maslow developed a theory of human behavior that gave us a concise model for understanding what motivates us. Most important, Maslow recognized that our most basic needs for survival and procreation must be met before we can address the higher-level needs most people aspire to in modern society. The relationship of these needs is most often represented by a stacked pyramid, as shown in Figure 2.2.

The way to understand this pyramid of needs is to start at the bottom. Without our basic needs met—food, water, shelter, and safety—people

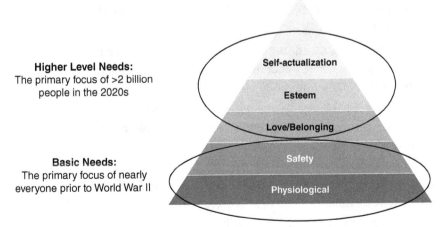

Figure 2.2   Maslow's Hierarchy of Needs

simply don't have the time to be motivated by love or a sense of belonging. Further, without a sense of love and belonging, most people are unable to develop a sense of esteem, the feeling of being well regarded and respected by others. Without esteem, self-actualization—the full realization of one's true potential as a human being—is impossible.

Maslow published his landmark theory in 1943 in the midst of World War II, and the huge reception it received was no accident. That terrible war destroyed cities, enabled the Holocaust, and ushered in the nuclear age. World War II cost tens of millions of lives. Its successful conclusion with the victory of the Allies created an unprecedented period of postwar prosperity and relative peace that lifted billions of people out of subsistence living into the higher rungs of Maslow's hierarchy.

Here's the point: The postwar economic expansion of 1946–2020 is what most of us alive today recognize as "normal." But it was not normal at all. It was unprecedented. Throughout almost the entirety of human history leading up to World War II, the vast majority of humanity eked out their existence on the bottom two rungs of Maslow's hierarchy. For 200,000 years of homo sapiens, there was simply no room in most people's short, hard lives for other pursuits.

As practitioners of wellness, we know that a few people have been pursuing Maslow's higher levels for centuries. We can point to the ancient healing arts of yoga, Ayurveda, Reiki, and traditional Chinese medicine, as well as the ancient roots of Western medicine and science, including Hippocrates, Galileo, da Vinci, and Newton, as evidence that people have existed at Maslow's higher levels for centuries.

We must remember, however, that these people were rare exceptions. In every case, they were either members of or closely connected to the elites of their day. Nearly everybody else in their day—more than 99.9 percent of humanity—lived at a bare subsistence level. Only in the past 100 years have their principles and discoveries been accessible to large portions of humanity.

That all began to change after World War II, when rapid advancements in science, engineering, education, health care, and food production began to lift tens of millions of people per year out of poverty and subsistence. That progression produced a steadily increasing number of middle-class and affluent people across the world, culminating in an historic "tipping point" in 2018, when for the first time in human history, there were more middle-class or affluent people than there were poor people (Brookings Institute, September 27, 2018).

This is important because it is the middle class and affluent who are afforded the opportunity to pursue the higher levels of Maslow's hierarchy, and chief among those is wellness. As the Brookings Institute points out:

Those in the middle class have some discretionary income. . . . They can afford to go to movies or indulge in other forms of entertainment. They may take vacations. And they are reasonably confident that they and their family can weather an economic shock—like illness or a spell of unemployment—without falling back into extreme poverty.

As we entered the 2020s, more than 4 billion people enjoyed this standard of living, and while the severe disruption of COVID-19 may indeed cause many to fall back economically for a time, the underlying postwar trend of rising living standards and reduced poverty will undoubtedly continue. It is important to embrace this truth for three reasons.

First, this truth helps us understand the massive expansion of wellness over the past forty years. The wellness movement is neither an accident nor a passing fad. It is the natural outcome of a societal imperative created by decades of rising living standards.

Second, this truth points to the massive growth opportunity in front of us. The wellness industry will most assuredly grow in the decade ahead, regardless of short-term recessions or other disruptions, and COVID-19 will inevitably act as an accelerant.

COVID-19 was a huge wakeup call in every nation on earth to improve the wellness of their populations. The impact of the virus and the societal disruptions it has caused have been terrible. The truth we must all face is that the worst outcomes and the most deaths have overwhelmingly occurred among those who were unwell to begin with. It turns out that biggest COVID-19 killer isn't the virus itself; it is the poor nutrition, sedentary lifestyles and stress that lead to the so called "preexisting conditions" of obesity, type II diabetes, cardiovascular disease, and cancer. This is what left so many people around the world unprepared to fight off the disease.

In addition, we have all simultaneously participated in an unprecedented social experiment. The months of sheltering at home and extreme social distancing required to combat the virus created secondary and tertiary impacts on all of us. In addition to so many small businesses impacted and so many jobs lost, we are all experiencing the mental, emotional and social impacts of sustained isolation. We have seen it in our loved ones and we have felt it in ourselves. Regardless of our age, socioeconomic status, or political leanings, we are all emerging from this crisis with a consensus around one point: That is no way to live!

In the wake of the pandemic that consensus will surely kick off a rennaissance of advancements in medical science and a broad social agreement that wellness is truly important. We can all find comfort in the knowledge that the next time a novel virus comes around we will far better prepared. At the same time, government and business leaders, public health officials, doctors, and healthcare workers will recognize the paramount importance of wellness. They will finally accept the inescapable truth that an ounce of wellness prevention is worth a pound of cure, and they will set into motion the policies and initiatives that address the root causes of the preventable diseases that made COVID-19 so much worse—sedentary lifestyles, poor nutrition, and stress. Wellness will therefore become a public health imperative for decades to come, and that will usher in a new age of wellness.

3 | The Generational Lens

While the numbers of middle-class and affluent people have been steadily growing for decades, their impact on the wellness industry has been only partially felt. This is because we humans are set in our ways. It takes at least one generation before rising economic standards translate into changed consumer behaviors, and two generations before those changes are fully realized.

Our attitudes and habits are largely determined by the world view set in our childhood. Therefore, an individual born into poverty who then climbs the economic ladder into the middle class or better will not easily move their motivations up Maslow's hierarchy of needs. Those first-generation middle-class individuals are much more likely to remain firmly rooted in a "safety" mindset.

We all have known people like that, classically characterized by epic work ethics and rigorous frugality. In North America, Western Europe, Australia, and New Zealand, these were the characteristics of the "Greatest Generation," those born in the 1910s and 1920s who came of age in the midst of the Great Depression of the 1930s and who helped win World War II. My grandmother was one of them

Genevieve Jackson Kiser became a widow when her husband—my grandfather—succumbed to pneumonia in 1936. She was left with four young children and no family support. Her oldest child, my mother, Sheila, was six years old at the time. For the rest of her life, my mom would recall her family being fed with a single scrawny chicken. Decades later, when the family would treat Grandma Kiser to a restaurant meal, she would embarrass us all by grabbing the sugar packets on the table and tucking them away in her giant purse.

At holiday and birthday parties, Grandma Kiser wouldn't let us throw away the wrapping paper. She would carefully smooth out each piece, fold it up, and tuck it into that same giant purse. We all learned to wrap our gifts loosely and use only minimal amounts of tape so the paper would not be destroyed in the unwrapping. When Grandma Kiser died in the early 1990s, she left a sizable estate to her children, accumulated through decades of hard work and careful saving. In the attic were boxes upon boxes of carefully folded wrapping paper.

Genevieve Kiser died an affluent woman, but she lived a very frugal life. She didn't travel, didn't buy nice cars, and refused to spend money on self-care. Later in life she wouldn't even pay the health insurance deductible to have her worn-out knees replaced. People like Grandma Kiser rarely joined health clubs, never visited boutique wellness studios, and wouldn't have dreamed of showing up at a spa.

But their children, grandchildren, and great-grandchildren sure did. This change of behavior and mindset started as the leading edge of the Baby Boom generation entered their third decade in the late 1970s. The rapid growth of wellness in the 1980s, 1990s, and 2000s can be tracked to the emergence of each successive postwar generation.

Although some dispute the precise cutoff years, the post–World War II generations are generally defined as follows:

Baby Boomers ("Boomers," born 1946–1964)
Generation X ("Gen-Xers," born 1965–1979)
Generation Y ("Millennials," born 1980–1996)
Generation Z ("Gen-Zers," born 1997 and after)

William Strauss and Neil Howe first conceived the theory of generational archetypes in their landmark 1991 book *Generations: A History of*

America's Future. Originally conceived as an American phenomenon, the archetypes have since been expanded to describe people of similar age groups throughout the developed world, in particular, Canada, the United Kingdom, Ireland, Western Europe, Australia, and New Zealand. These regions comprise most of the wellness movement of the past 40 years, and more than 90 percent of Mindbody's wellness business customers are located in these regions.

Generational archetypes can describe only the norms of a generation; they don't describe everybody. For every member of a given generation who fits the archetype, one can easily point to others who do not. Nevertheless, the correlation between the leading-edge members of each successive generation reaching their 30s, the age when most people become conscious of the need for wellness, and the corresponding waves of our industry's growth is truly compelling.

By combining this generational lens with our understanding of Maslow's hierarchy of needs and the progression of information technology, we can identify the forces that fueled our industry's astounding growth from 1980 to 2020. That knowledge can then give us a lens through which to make reliable predictions of what the future holds for our industry. While the COVID-19 thunderbolt has caused severe disruption in many wellness business categories, it did not change human nature. Neither did it change the societal forces that will fuel the next wave of wellness industry growth in the decade ahead. If anything, COVID-19 has only accelerated it.

The wellness industry as we know it today began in 1980 and grew in three distinct waves, each larger, more far reaching, and more beneficial than the last. The First Wave was driven by Baby Boomers and enabled by personal computers, the Second Wave was driven by Generation X and enabled by the Internet, and the Third Wave was driven by Millennials and enabled by smartphones and cloud technology.

The First Wave of Wellness (1980–1996): Boomer-Driven and PC-Enabled

Baby Boomers largely grew up during a period marked by rapidly rising living standards, stable households, and unprecedented prosperity. Boomers were therefore the first generation in human history to easily move up Maslow's hierarchy of needs. Classically idealistic, judgmental, and energetic, no prior generation has left such a deep impact on our culture and economy, because none had included so many people raised in the absence of poverty or hunger.

The Boomers are at once polarized and polarizing. We've all heard the stories of their idealism and narcissism in the 1960s and 1970s—the civil rights movement, the Summer of Love, Woodstock, and anti–Vietnam War protests. Less known but equally valid are stories of heroism and valor—soldiers, sailors, and marines who bravely fought in the Vietnam War. With the eldest of this generation now approaching their eighth decade of life, Boomers still dominate both the Right and Left of the political debate. It is no surprise that they have held the office of president or prime minister of nearly every developed country on earth for more than 30 years. Classically contentious throughout their lives, Baby Boomers did largely agree in the 1980s on two objectives: healthy living and making money. Those two focus areas would ignite an explosion of health and fitness, which we now call the *First Wave* of the wellness movement.

The First Wave is when the health food industry took off, when *Self* and *Men's Health* magazines began, when racquet sports reached their peak popularity, and when long-distance running, cycling, and triathlons became all the rage. These were also the years when Jane Fonda, Richard Simmons, and a few others made fortunes selling workout videos, leveraging a new technology of videotape to introduce millions to group exercise.

In the 1970s the fitness industry had consisted mostly of small sweaty gyms designed for body builders, as well as YMCAs and JCCs focused mainly on youth sports. In the 1980s, the industry innovated to meet rising Boomer demand, catering to both men and women; they incorporated group exercise classes, swimming, and racket sports, and leveraged the leading technology of the day—personal computing—to scale like never before.

The International Health and Racquet Sports Association (IHRSA) was established in 1981, and the first health club software providers emerged a few years later to help automate the nascent industry of full-service clubs. The earliest software solutions were PC applications focused on automating the authorization and settlement of large numbers of recurring credit card and direct debit transactions. Automated member management enabled health clubs to scale, and within a few years thousands of new large full-service clubs opened their doors.

In the early 1980s, Mark Mastrov founded 24 Hour Fitness, Donohue Wildman founded Bally's Health Club, Louis Welch founded LA Fitness, and David Lloyd opened his first eponymous gym in Hertfordshire, England. A few years later, Doug Levine founded Crunch Fitness and Vito Errico founded Equinox. The First Wave of wellness also fueled an explosion of innovative workout equipment, including Precor, Stairmaster, Cybex, and Nautilus. It also planted the seeds of the boutique fitness movement that would dominate the Second and Third Waves to come, central among these being the emergence in the early 1990s of three distinctive types of independent group exercises: Pilates, yoga, and Spinning®.

Joseph Pilates began teaching his method in New York City in the 1930s and 1940s. Designed initially to help professional dancers avoid and recover from injury, Pilates did not expand into the general population until innovative entrepreneurs began to expand the practice in the early 1990s. One of those early innovators was Mari Winsor, who opened her first Beverly Hills studio in 1990 and soon became known as "The Pilates Teacher to the Stars." In the years that followed, Mari would introduce Pilates to millions of Americans through her TV infomercials and DVDs. Mari's innovative spirit and indomitable energy would later inspire thousands of future studio owners and hundreds of thousands of teachers who would change the lives of millions of people in the decades to come.

Similarly, the practice of yoga had been imported from India to the West decades prior. The teachings of this ancient practice were largely restricted to institutes, ashrams, and retreat centers. Yoga did not become accessible to the general public until a new wave of innovative neighborhood yoga studios opened their doors and began to accept drop-in students. Early yoga business innovators included Sharon Gannon and David Life, who founded Jivamukti Yoga in 1984; Maty Ezraty and Chuck Miller, who founded Yogaworks in 1987; and Gurmukh and Gurushabd Khalsa, who founded Golden Bridge Yoga in 1992. As with Pilates, these early yoga innovators and hundreds more like them would inspire thousands of yoga entrepreneurs and hundreds of thousands of teachers. Yoga would become a truly global phenomenon in the 2000s, and in the 2010s it would be imported back into India as wellness took hold in that rapidly advancing economy.

At the same time, an entirely new group exercise method in the 1990s would have a transformational impact on the boutique fitness movement in the decades to follow. In 1994, Johnny G and John Baudhin founded Mad Dogg Sports to accelerate the adoption of their invention—Spinning®, which vastly improved on the stationary bikes of the day and lent itself to a group exercise delivery method. First implemented in health clubs and later in neighborhood studios, Spinning® would inspire multiple offshoot indoor cycling brands and become the foundation of the first live streaming at-home delivery model—Peloton®.

The First Wave of wellness is also when therapeutic massage and other spa treatments began to move outside of the luxury resorts and retreat centers where they had flourished for decades and into more accessible neighborhood day spas. The Day Spa Association was formed in 1988 and the International Spa Association (iSPA) in 1992 to serve that nascent industry. In addition, the first small studios offering the ancient wellness practices of acupuncture, Ayurveda, Chinese medicine, Tae Chi Qigong, and Reiki emerged during this time.

In short, the Boomer-led First Wave of wellness created a vibrant industry where none had existed before. First Wave entrepreneurs applied new thinking to age-old practices and leveraged the latest technologies—personal computers, videotapes, and DVDs—to reach millions of people and stimulate decades of massive growth. All of this laid the groundwork for the next wave, which would be even larger and more impactful.

The Second Wave of Wellness (1997–2010): Gen-X-Driven and Internet-Enabled

In the mid-1990s, the first cohorts of Generation X reached their 30s and began to adopt wellness practices alongside their Boomer elders, and before long they began to reshape the industry with their decidedly different personalities.

The Gen-X personality is commonly characterized as more independent, individualistic, and pragmatic than Boomers. Blake Beltram and I are Gen-Xers, and we know their experiences and personalities well. We experienced the social upheavals of the 1960s and 1970s as children, and became adults in the time of the AIDS epidemic. Often called the "latchkey generation," we were far more likely than Boomers to have divorced or dual-income-earning parents. We encountered drugs and alcohol at an earlier age and witnessed the excesses of our Boomer causes and ideologies first-hand. Growing up faster and harder than our Boomer elders, Gen-Xers are classically more skeptical and independent-minded. These characteristics make us more entrepreneurial as well.

Whereas the First Wave of wellness was characterized by homogenized brands and large, multi-purpose health clubs, the Gen-X-led Second Wave was driven by specialized practices and locally authentic independent studios. These smaller-footprint businesses had a key feature of much lower startup costs and significantly less financial risk than the Boomer-led health clubs. In the late 1990s, thousands of Gen-X-led yoga, Pilates, and indoor cycling studios began to spring up, providing their trailing-edge Boomer and Gen-X clientele with more personalized wellness experiences.

Due to their smaller scale, these smaller studio businesses could not afford the expensive client-server software that had been created for health clubs, and that software didn't meet their specialized scheduling, client, and staff management needs anyway. Therefore, for the first several years of the Second Wave, most of these early boutique wellness studios ran on pencil and paper, which restricted their ability to grow. That technology gap would become the opportunity that Blake Beltram and I founded Mindbody to address in 2000.

At first, the operators of large health clubs saw the boutique wellness movement with a blend of dismissiveness and curiosity. In 2005, the first year that Mindbody had a booth at the annual IHRSA conference, the preeminent fitness industry event of the day, there were no other boutique wellness brands represented in the exposition hall. We were such an oddity that the conference staff misunderstood the online nature of our software and misspelled our company name. Our badges and the trade show guide described us as "mind and body on the line." We spent that first conference explaining to bemused health club operators that we were in fact a Cloud software company. Their ambivalence toward us and the boutique wellness movement would soon change.

A few years later, a successful health club operator approached me at our IHRSA booth and complained, "Thanks to you, dozens of these little fitness studios have popped up to steal all my members. I feel like Gulliver being surrounded by the Lilliputians!"

That club operator's experience and response reflected a transition happening all over the globe. Changing consumer tastes and a disruptive technology had fueled a shift in the wellness industry. Tens of thousands of boutique fitness studios had emerged, leveraging the latest technologies of the day to provide a more compelling customer experience at a fraction of the cost. It would be several more years before a significant number of club operators would begin to shift their business models, while many of them would linger in Elisabeth Kübler-Ross's first two stages of grief—denial and anger.

During the Second Wave of wellness our world was hit with multiple crises—the dot-com bust and recession of the early 2000s, the 9/11 attacks and War on Terror, the Financial Crisis of 2007 and 2008, and the long, slow recovery of 2009–2010. Rather than slowing the Second Wave down, each of these challenges actually stimulated wellness industry innovation and growth.

In each of these crises, millions more people faced with increased stress and reduced household incomes de-prioritized big-ticket purchases and prioritized self-care, social connections, and affordable luxuries. Crises fueled more demand for wellness services.

Meanwhile, on the business side, corporate layoffs caused tens of thousands of new wellness entrepreneurs to enter the market with new businesses. At Mindbody, we called these people the "Corporate Refugees," and their energy, resources, and business acumen vastly increased the supply of high-quality local wellness experiences. Several of the boutique brands launched by corporate refugees would go on to become some of the most successful wellness brands we know today (see Figure 3.1).

As these well-known brands prove, crises present opportunities, and you don't have to wait for good times to launch a successful business. In fact, times of recession and strife are the best times to launch an innovative brand.

The Second Wave of wellness firmly established the boutique wellness movement, greatly expanding the size, diversity, and positive impact of the industry. That set the stage for a third and even larger wave of wellness,

Brand	Year Founded		Brand	Year Founded
The Bar Method	2001		Pure Yoga	2001
D1 Training	2001		Corepower Yoga	2002
Exhale	2003		Modo Yoga	2004
spavia	2005		Elements Therapeutic Massage	2006
LaVida Massage	2007		Massage Addict	2008
Barre3	2008		Oxygen Yoga & Fitness	2008
The Camp Boot Camp	2008		iLoveKickboxing	2009
Orangetheory Fitness	2010		F45 Training	2011

Figure 3.1   Examples of Successful Wellness Brands, 2001–2010

fueled by the proliferation of smartphones and other connected devices, and the emergence of the largest wellness-oriented generation yet.

The Third Wave of Wellness (2011–2020): Millennials, Smartphones, and Cloud Technology

In the early 2010s, as large numbers of 20- and 30-something Millennials began to enter the workforce, they adopted boutique wellness practices more rapidly and in greater numbers than Gen-Xers and Boomers. As the older generations were still fully engaged, this Third Wave was almost completely additive to the industry.

Millennials are more globally connected and massive in numbers than any previous generation. Coming of age concurrently with the emergence of global high-speed Internet, cloud computing, and powerful smartphones, the Millennial generation is the first to truly think globally. You can speak with tech Millennials in India, China, Japan, and the other developed countries of Asia-Pacific, Europe, and Latin America, and you will find they have more in common with each other than they do with the older generations in their own countries.

Millennials prioritize experiences and social connections over material possessions. They experienced 9/11 as children and the Great Recession as young adults. They grew up with the War on Terror and saw their parents' nest eggs decimated by the real estate crash in 2008–2009. They also attended college in greater numbers and took on more student debt than any previous generation. Many of them struggled to launch their careers during the slow economic recovery of the early 2010s. These formative experiences shaped the Millennial mind, giving them a strong aversion to financial risk and big-ticket purchases. There are plenty of Millennial entrepreneurs, particularly in technology, but as a percentage of their total numbers, this generation has started far fewer businesses than Gen-X-ers or Baby Boomers. This may change in the decade ahead, but so far the classic Millennial would much rather spend discretionary income on low-budget travel and regular boutique wellness experiences than take on debt to buy a home or launch a business.

Millennials also have a strong affinity for globalism, environmental causes, and social justice. Millennials are deeply concerned about climate change and economic inequality. This is the generation that fueled Senator Bernie Sanders's presidential bids, propelled the legalization of gay marriage, and expanded the movement to recognize broad-based LGBTQ+ rights.

Millennials love variety and authenticity. They have an affinity for local and authentic crafts, foods, and experiences. In short, more Millennials align with the principles and ethos of the wellness movement than Baby Boomers and Gen-X-ers combined.

In the 2010s the wellness industry began to morph to meet Millennial tastes. The decade saw the emergence of whole new categories of boutique wellness classes and services, including BootCamp-style workouts and High Intensity Interval Training (HIIT), along with a resurgence of indoor cycling, led by Soul Cycle, FlyWheel, Rush Cycle, Cyclebar, and others. The three largest boutique fitness brands—Crossfit®, Orangetheory Fitness, and F45 Training—took off in the 2010s, fueled largely by Millennial passion for the tribe-like atmosphere they provide.

Meanwhile, whole new categories of wellness businesses emerged, offering specialized services such as salt room therapies, meditation classes, cryotherapy, intravenous hydration therapy, and boutique beauty and grooming. We can thank Millennials for the cool new hipster barbershops that specialized in classic men's coifs, straight razor shaves, and epic beards, as well as for the proliferation of blow dry bars, nail salons, and lash bars.

All of this differentiation and growth was enabled by iPhones and Android smartphones, unlimited data plans, and the emergence of cloud-enabled technologies.

Yelp went public in 2009 and rapidly expanded the inventory of wellness business reviews in the 2010s. ClassPass and the Mindbody app were both released in 2013, enabling aggregate searching and booking of wellness classes and appointments, and Google released Reserve with Google in 2016, enabling seamless search, discovery, and booking of wellness classes and appointments. In 2017, both Mindbody and ClassPass released dynamic pricing to the wellness businesses they serve, enabling pricing to discount or surge according to local supply and demand.

At the same time, the ability to connect heart rate monitors and exercise machine outputs enabled boutique fitness studios to offer a new form of immersive experience. Innovators such as Fitmetrix, which was founded in 2013 and acquired by Mindbody in 2018, leveraged cloud technologies to greatly reduce the cost of deploying these capabilities in studios. At the same time, innovators such as Peloton®, founded in 2012, and Mirror®, founded in 2016, leveraged the same equipment and cloud technologies to bring connected fitness and group exercise into people's homes.

Collectively, these technological advancements helped to further expand, globalize, and democratize the Third Wave of wellness. By the end of the decade, one could just as easily find a boutique wellness studio in Prague, Bangalore, and Shanghai as they could in Los Angeles, New York, London, or Sydney. And, when someone walked into that studio, they would most likely encounter clientele representing all three postwar generations. Wellness had indeed gone mainstream and global, and was worth more than $4.5 trillion in 2019.

And then COVID-19 hit.

4

The Future of Wellness in a Post-COVID World

COVID-19 interrupted the Third Wave of wellness. Without a global disaster of this magnitude, the Third Wave would have continued deep into the 2020s, fueled by ever greater numbers of Millennials entering their peak spending years and the continued strong engagement of Gen-Xers and aging Baby Boomers.

Virtual wellness offerings would have expanded and improved gradually throughout the decade with superior accessibility and affordability. Larger and better on-demand and live-streaming content combined with ever-improving and less expensive connected devices would have further expanded and democratized the overall wellness market. This would have siphoned only a portion of the growth that might otherwise have gone to face-to-face experiences at the brick-and-mortar studios.

As late as January 2020, Mindbody's research found that most early adopters of home-based virtual wellness—including those who favored the sophisticated connected offerings from Peloton® and Mirror®—were adopting those tools to supplement their workouts in the brick-and-mortar studios, not replace them. Meanwhile, the proliferating appointment-based wellness businesses, from therapeutic massage to boutique beauty and grooming, were well on their way to booking their best quarter ever, providing services that could not be delivered through a screen.

As we moved further into the decade of the 2020s these forces, combined with the emergence of leading-edge Gen-Zers, would have given the Third Wave of wellness a final push of growth before teeing up a graceful transition to an even more exciting Fourth Wave to follow.

But that story is transpiring in some parallel universe we don't live in.

In our reality, COVID-19 hit our industry in March 2020 like a thunderbolt, and the transition to the next wave will be sooner and more jarring. The pandemic instantly and prematurely ended the Third Wave of wellness before the Fourth Wave had a chance to fully develop and set up. This idled millions of wellness practitioners and caused tens of thousands of wellness businesses to fail during the long months of shelter at home and excruciatingly slow reopening. In the recovery that followed, only a portion of the wellness practitioners who had been fully employed prior to COVID-19 would return to work for the same businesses, and tens of thousands of brick-and-mortar wellness businesses would fail.

The unexpected shock of the COVID-19 pandemic also kicked off a rapid acceleration of industry innovation. Within days of the first shelter-at-home orders, thousands of wellness businesses were offering virtual experiences to their clients via off-the-shelf tools like Zoom, Facebook, Instagram, and YouTube. Within a month, Mindbody had accelerated the release of our long-awaited integrated Virtual Wellness Platform, enabling wellness business owners to build scalable virtual businesses in conjunction with their brick-and-mortar offerings. In the months that followed, multiple other business management solutions followed suit. Necessity had indeed proven to be the mother of invention.

So, what does the future hold? First, we must acknowledge that you and I are engaging through a time machine. You are reading or listening to these words several months or even years after I have written them. Therefore, you already know things that I cannot possibly have known when I wrote this.

For example:

1. Who will take the oath of office in January 2021 as president of the United States?

2. When will COVID-19 prophylactic and therapeutic drugs be developed and widely distributed?

3. When will we have a safe and effective vaccine?

4. How deep will the COVID-19 recession be and how long will it last?

5. Which regions of the world will be more economically impacted?

Fortunately, these temporal factors are largely irrelevant to the long-term future of the wellness industry. Instead, certain longer-term truths are far more likely to determine the future of wellness, and armed with those truths we can make some observations.

Here are seven post-COVID societal truths that transcend political leaders, the economy, and the pandemic response and fifteen wellness industry predictions for the future.

Truth #1: COVID-19 has laid bare the true societal costs of obesity, sedentary lifestyles and poor nutrition.

Prediction #1: People's desire to improve their physical well-being will be greatly amplified by the COVID-19 pandemic. At the same time, more employers, insurance companies, and governments will embrace the preventive benefits and increase their subsidies, incentives, and educational campaigns to activate millions of people into healthier and happier lifestyles. This will fuel massive wellness industry growth.

Truth #2: Sheltering at home and social distancing have amplified the need for services that support emotional and social well-being.

Prediction #2: The demand for mind and body practices, massage therapy, and meditation will increase, especially for home delivery models.

Truth #3: Prolonged sheltering at home and the accelerated adoption of work from home and hybrid work options have amplified people's hunger to get out of the house.

Prediction #3: As business, education, and government organizations reduce their reliance on commercial office space, the demand for wellness services in those commercial zones will go down. This will harm businesses in those neighborhoods.

Prediction #4: At the same time, reduced demand for commercial office space will increase commercial office space vacancies and decrease commercial rent rates, creating opportunities for new residential developments and brick-and-mortar wellness businesses to emerge.

Prediction #5: Increased adoption of work from home and virtual meetings will increase the value people place on offline interaction and group activities in their leisure time. This will fuel demand for wellness services in those neighborhoods. growth of outdoor wellness activities, as well as wellness businesses located in residential neighborhoods.

Truth #4: Sheltering at home has taught everyone to interact virtually.

Prediction #6: The principal advantages of virtual wellness are convenience, cost, and physical safety. Less obvious and even more important is emotional safety; people will be able to avoid the body shame and embarrassment they may feel when they have their first face-to-face wellness experience. Millions of people will now be free to more easily sample and adopt compelling virtual experiences.

Prediction #7: Most brick-and-mortar wellness businesses will become hybrid wellness businesses, leveraging their virtual extensions to reach larger audiences and draw more people into the offline face-to-face experience.

Prediction #8: Brick-and-mortar wellness businesses without virtual extensions will find it difficult to survive.

Truth #5: The pandemic has made billions of people more concerned about sanitation, hygiene, and social distancing.

Prediction #9: People will be choosier about the people they socialize with. This will be a challenge for large multi-purpose health clubs and low-cost/high-volume 24-hour gyms.

Prediction #10: People will be willing to pay a higher premium for wellness experiences that involve fewer people. This will be a boon for personal trainers and high-end boutiques that serve a more affluent clientele.

Prediction #11: Tribalism will increase. Aggregation platforms that fill classes with last-minute strangers will be less desired.

Truth #6: Connected devices are rapidly becoming more commonplace and affordable.

Prediction #12: High-quality video feeds, heart rate monitoring, and workout machine tracking will make a high-quality connected wellness experience accessible to hundreds of millions of middle-income and lower-income people. This will help drive the resurgence of local practitioners who offer authenticity, community, and the option for hybrid online and offline experiences.

Prediction #13: Peloton® and Mirror® will soon find their offerings commoditized by hundreds of thousands of connected independent practitioners, who can offer a more personal online and offline experience.

Truth #7: People are living longer and expecting a higher quality of life in their older years.

Prediction #14: Rapid advancements in medical science and public health, combined with the increased adoption of wellness practices, will vastly increase average lifespans. Most of us alive today will reasonably expect to remain active well into our 90s. Millennials and Gen-Zers can expect to live well into their 100s.

Prediction #15: Wellness practices for seniors will grow massively in the decades ahead.

What does all the above add up to? Wellness remains the largest and most important opportunity of our age; the industry will experience even more growth and innovation due to COVID-19. If you understand what is happening and have what it takes, you could not have picked a better time to launch a wellness business.

PART II

Prepare Yourself for a Hero's Journey

5

First Things First: Identify What You Love, Get Certified, and Work in the Industry

The fact that you picked up this book suggests you aren't truly fulfilled working for others. You may have the vision to deliver wellness in an entirely new way. Your soul may feel crushed by corporate bureaucracy and possess an instinctive understanding of which work activities create value and which do not. You may yearn to create a company culture that fills people's spirits and makes work fun. Or perhaps you simply yearn for the independence and the freedom that comes from being your own boss.

Or maybe you are like me and you feel driven by all a combination of all the above. These traits are the hallmarks of an aspiring entrepreneur and, regardless of where you are coming from, your first steps to set yourself up for future success are to identify what you love, get certified, and gain real-world experience working in that branch of the wellness industry.

Identify What You Love

The first step in preparing yourself for the journey ahead is to discover the wellness modality you truly love. Maybe it's yoga, Pilates, indoor cycling, or group exercise class. Maybe it's guided meditation, therapeutic massage, or energy work. Maybe it's a particular category of spa or salon services. Whatever it is, if you truly love it, you will find yourself seeking out that experience over and over again. You will be drawn to others in the field and you will enjoy reading about the practice and learning from others in the field. Other practitioners will notice your passion and accumulating skills. The true mark that you've found it is when people start saying, "You should do this!" When that happens and your heart leaps, then you've reached the first milestone in creating a wellness business that matters: identifying something you can be truly great at.

Get Certified and Start Working

The next step is to find out what it takes to become certified in the practice or modality you have identified. Most of these certification programs take less than a year and many can be done in a few months. This is something most people can do while keeping their day jobs, and I have met thousands of people over the past who have done so.

If you plan to start a yoga or fitness business, you should become a certified teacher, trainer, or coach in that modality and work for others for at least two years—gaining hundreds of hours with actual paying clients practicing your craft.

If you plan to open a spa, you should become a licensed massage therapist or esthetician. If you are going to practice acupuncture, traditional Chinese medicine, chiropractic or Ayurvedic medicine, esthetics, or cosmetology, you will be required by law to complete a rigorous education and become licensed. Most of these licenses are transferrable, but the rules vary by state and always involve time and money. If you have not already started down the licensure path, you can remove one obstacle by choosing a school in the state and near the city you plan to practice in.

Don't skip this essential step. There is no substitute for becoming certified or licensed in your craft and gaining hundreds or even thousands of hours of direct client experience. This practice will teach you thousands of nuances that can be learned only by doing, will help you formulate your own compelling and unique experience design, and will give you the relevancy to run your wellness business and lead others later. All of these things are essential to your future success.

We won't list all the ways to get certified or licensed. That information is dynamic and easily discoverable by searching online. The point is to do it. As a wellness entrepreneur, you have much to do and much to learn. There is no more effective way to kick off that learning than to work in the industry. Do it!

When Your Enthusiasm Peters Out, Try Something Else

While you are studying and working toward your certification or license, you may discover that the wellness practice you thought you loved isn't so compelling. You may lose interest or decide to shift to something else that has caught your attention. That is part of the journey and is perfectly okay. Leverage your head, heart, and gut to find the one thing that truly lights you up. It is far easier and less costly to change directions now than it will be down the road.

6

Five Essential Traits of Successful Wellness Entrepreneurs

Success in the wellness industry is not about where you came from, what you look like, or how you were raised. Successful wellness entrepreneurs are like successful entrepreneurs in any industry: they come from every ethnic group, socioeconomic background, and sexual identity. Some are blessed by life with natural advantages, such as a strong supportive family or natural excellence in academics, sports, or the arts. Many others aren't so blessed. In fact, if you study the most successful entrepreneurs of the past 200 years, from J. D. Rockefeller and Henry Ford to Steve Jobs and Oprah Winfrey, you'll find that these unique individuals are just as likely to be born with none of those supposed "advantages." Many were born with little in the form of material wealth and many others had learning disabilities. Others came of age facing discrimination and persecution for their ethnic heritage or sexual identity. For example, Oprah Winfrey was born to an unwed teenaged housemaid in 1950s Mississippi.

For entrepreneurs, it doesn't matter where we came from because entrepreneurialism is the ultimate meritocracy. The ability to create something out of nothing, to go "from 0 to 1," requires a unique blend of talent, skill, and pure gumption. Whereas the conscious and unconscious biases of others may prevent someone who lacks the "right" education, upbringing, or socioeconomic background from achieving their greatest success working for others, there are only two groups of people you need to impress as an entrepreneur: your customers and your investors.

Customers don't care where you came from or what school you went to. All they care about is the quality of the products and experiences you provide them. Think about the last amazing wellness experience you received. Did you review the résumé of the wellness professional who led the class or delivered the service? Did you inquire into the socioeconomic background or education of the business owner? Of course not. The only thing that mattered to you was the exceptional experience you received and the value you attached to that experience.

Smart investors bet on capability and performance, not résumés. Their dollars will follow your demonstrated ability to earn a profit delivering compelling products and experiences to lots of customers. Everything else is irrelevant.

Most of the rest of this book is focused on how to design and deliver those compelling products and services in a scalable way. Before we dive into that, however, let's get real and talk about whether you are the right person to do it.

Over the past twenty years, the Mindbody team has worked with and served tens of thousands of wellness entrepreneurs, from the highly successful to the utterly incapable. The successful ones come in all shapes and sizes, various personality types, and every possible background. What made them successful, and I believe would make them successful in any entrepreneurial pursuit, are five essential personality traits of successful entrepreneurs—characteristics you must uncover and develop in yourself before you proceed with your business plans:

1. **Authentic Enthusiasm:** A great passion and zeal for what your business will deliver, informed by actual experience
2. **Grit:** The ability to sustain your enthusiasm and strengthen your commitment when faced with inevitable setbacks
3. **Agile Thinking:** The habit of alternately zooming your focus in on the key details of your business and zooming out to stay in touch with the big picture

4. **Effective Decision Making:** The habit of routinely leveraging your head, heart, and gut to make great decisions
5. **Adaptability:** The willingness to adjust your approach when faced with new realities

Essential Trait #1: Authentic Enthusiasm

Your enthusiasm for your profession, your business, and wellness in general is the energy in your battery. It's what lights you up, drives your actions, and influences others. In addition, the authentic enthusiasm an entrepreneur creates is the magnetic attraction that pulls in the customers, partners, team members, and investors needed to succeed. Entrepreneurs' enthusiasm for their business won't guarantee their success, but a lack of enthusiasm will most definitely prevent it.

This does not mean you have to be extroverted, bubbly, highly social, or even likable to build a successful wellness business. Some of the most famously successful entrepreneurs in history were classically introverted. Many were difficult to get to know, awkward in conversation, uncomfortable in front of audiences, and even challenging to work with. But, despite their social awkwardness, these exceptional entrepreneurs were able to conceive brilliant original business models, engage with customers, and attract talented people because they possessed deep expertise and unique insights in their fields and they cultivated authentic enthusiasm around that.

This reinforces the essential steps outlined in Chapter 5. You must know your craft and understand your customers. Without knowledge, your enthusiasm will be inauthentic, and when it comes to our time, our money, and our wellness, nothing repels people faster than a lack of authenticity.

So, treat the time you invest getting certified and working in the wellness industry as a golden opportunity to deepen your authentic enthusiasm. This will charge your battery, giving you an important reserve for the challenging road ahead.

Essential Trait #2: Grit

If your enthusiasm is the energy in your battery, your grit represents the size and durability of that battery. So what is grit and how do we know if we have it? Angela Lee Duckworth has written and spoken extensively about grit, and this quote from her book *Grit* summarizes it nicely:

Grit is sticking with your future. Day in and day out. Not just for the week. Not just for the month. But for years. And, working really hard to make that future a reality. Grit is living life like it's a marathon not a sprint.

I would add that grit includes a healthy dose of courage—the courage to face your challenges and take needed actions, to do things that really scare you.

One example of a gritty wellness entrepreneur is Alexandra Bonetti Perez. A Venezuelan immigrant, Alexandra repeatedly encountered the subtle and not so subtle biases of white men as she was launching her highly successful New York boutique fitness business, Bari Studios, in the 2010s. Alexandra recounts an exchange with her landlord:

I walked into a meeting with my landlord to renegotiate my rent, and he says, 'Why didn't you bring your dad or your husband to this meeting?' I replied, 'They're busy and they don't work with me, but I'll think about that for our next meeting.'

Many people faced with such blatant sexism would have quickly angered. They might have yelled and stormed out of the office. They might have engaged in a long and distracting attempt to correct his world view, or they might have been emotionally crushed. Alexandra did none of those things. Instead, she focused on her objective—renegotiating her lease on more favorable terms—and she taught the landlord a lesson at the same time. In her next meeting with the landlord, Alexandra simply paid her Uber driver to come to the meeting and introduced him as her "male business associate." He, of course, contributed nothing to the meeting, but Alexandra got the lease terms she wanted.

That's gritty!

Gritty people channel sleights or insults into constructive action.

Gritty people easily lose themselves in challenging tasks for weeks or months at a time. They enjoy working hard—especially when that work is meaningful.

Gritty people don't concern themselves with near-term rewards or recognition. Their drive comes from a focus on long-term goals.

Gritty people are energized by setbacks. Instead of asking themselves why something bad just happened, they ask themselves what that situation requires of them.

Gritty people have the confidence to faithfully follow their own internal compass and are not overly concerned with the opinions of others.

Gritty people are resilient. When they get knocked down, they get back up.

Gritty people are courageous. It's not that they don't feel pain or fear. It's that they are able to quickly shake it off, reconnect to their purpose, and get back to work.

I believe grit is a natural human capability that can surface in every human being. So why do so many people tire of challenging tasks, becoming demoralized or losing interest when faced with difficulty? In my observation, the people with low grit levels are either living the wrong life or fixated on false narratives. Both causes are recoverable.

Developing Your Grit

The first requirement to unblock one's grit is developing a sense of self-worth—a deep belief in one's value as a human being, coupled with an understanding that we are each deserving of our own happiness and responsible for creating it. If you didn't gain this sense of empowerment and self-worth in childhood, you will need to develop it before you can be successful as an entrepreneur. Start by reading or listening to *The Seven Habits of Highly Effective People*, by Stephen Covey. That book will change your life.

Then read or watch stories of people who inspire you, especially those who overcame great obstacles to make a difference. These are the heroes' journeys that inspire us all—Abraham Lincoln, Harriet Tubman, Winston Churchill, Nelson Mandela, Maya Angelou. It wasn't their heroic natures that enabled their journeys. It was their journeys that made them heroic.

The second requirement to unblock your grit is to foster a deep appreciation for the virtue of hard work. Nothing meaningful in life is easy. Whether you are achieving a fitness goal, learning to rock climb, perfecting a yoga pose, or starting a business, you have to do the work. And the most meaningful things require the most work.

When you are working on things that matter most, the effort shouldn't deplete you. If your job is sucking the life from you, if you truly hate

Mondays and "Thank God It's Friday" is how you feel most of the time, then you are in the wrong job. Change it!

Or perhaps the issue is more personal than that. Maybe you are in the wrong relationship or running a life script that someone else wrote. Your soul is crying out for a change. People questioning their own sexual orientation or gender identity face these issues. The LGBTQ+ movement has not only righted a diversity, equality, and inclusivity ("DEI") wrong, it has empowered millions of people to live their best lives and contribute more fully to humanity.

At Mindbody we have a robust DEI movement with multiple affinity groups. We have witnessed firsthand countless people simultaneously improving their lives and becoming more effective professionals by exercising their ultimate freedom to be who they truly are. This is the essence of the top two tiers of Maslow's hierarchy of needs—esteem and self-actualization—and it is essential to becoming a successful entrepreneur.

Whatever your life history and circumstances, recognizing the grit blockers in your life and having the courage to remove those blockers to become who you truly are will strengthen your grit and improve your life.

This important habit of listening to your heart and gut and addressing the grit blockers in your life isn't selfish. It is an empowering act of love, and when done from a place of authenticity it ultimately serves to improve the lives of everyone around you. And that has everything to do with building a wellness business that lasts.

Essential Trait #3: Agile Thinking

There is a subtle but important thinking habit that every successful entrepreneur possesses. They have the unique ability to alternately dive into the details of their business and then come back out and see the big picture, and then dive back into check the details.

Using the metaphor of a telephoto lens on a high-quality camera, successful entrepreneurs are constantly moving the zoom feature of their camera back and forth. They "zoom in" to understand the important details of their business, and they "zoom back out" to relate those details to the big picture—industry trends, consumer behavior, and competition, for example—and then zoom back in to check the details again. Successful entrepreneurs do this constantly, and it is a special form of mental agility.

The most important aspect of this trait is not to let your mind get stuck in either the zoomed-in or zoomed-out state. There is failure in both places. Imagine entrepreneurs inspired by the wellness revolution. They spend all their time reading, talking, and advocating for it, but while they are doing this, they are ignoring the key metrics of their business. They aren't tracking attendance, retention, staff performance, revenue, and expenses. Their business could be failing and they are blissfully unaware, until their bookkeeper calls and says they need $20,000 to make Wednesday's payroll.

Or imagine the opposite scenario. Wellness entrepreneurs are immersed in their numbers, studying, analyzing, and worrying about them constantly. But they are not paying attention to how the industry and consumer tastes are evolving. They are not reading the trade journals and websites, they are not sampling competitor experiences, and they are not talking to customers and other business owners. Even if currently profitable, their business will eventually run into problems.

You have to do both. Constantly. That is mental agility, and you can develop the habit with practice.

Developing Mental Agility

To develop the habit of mental agility, first assess which frame of mind you most easily operate in. When you think or talk about the business of wellness, do you spend more time zoomed out, thinking about the big problems of society and trends in the industry, or do you spend more time zoomed in on the details of how you will make a living delivering wellness in your community? Where your mind more easily goes is your preferred frame of mind, and you can think of that like writing with your dominant hand. It's your easiest and most effective mode.

What if you injured that hand and had to learn to write with the other? How would you learn that? By doing it, of course. Our minds are like our muscles, and we can strengthen them through effort and practice. At this point in the book, I have been writing for several months and I am about halfway through the journey. This has already consumed hundreds of hours of my spare time, while still serving as the CEO of Mindbody. I can tell you that the effort has significantly improved my written and verbal communication skills and made me more effective in my job. The same is true for virtually any worthwhile endeavor. When we engage our minds to do something hard, our minds get stronger. This is true whether you are mastering the guitar or becoming a better business professional. Practice makes perfect.

Zooming in to focus on the details

If you are one of the naturally zoomed-out people, commit now to spending several hours per week for the next several months studying the details of your future business. Here is a homework assignment to get you started:
Zoom-In Muscle Builder

1. Learn how to create a spreadsheet in Google Sheets or Excel by watching a 10–15-minute tutorial on YouTube. If you don't already have a preference, I recommend Google Sheets. It's free and easily shared with others.
2. Do a spreadsheet analysis of average wellness prices in your neighborhood by Google searching for all the businesses of similar type. For example, for a fitness studio, it would look something like this:

	Drop-in Price	5-Class Card	10-Class Card	Monthly Unlimited	Intro Offer
Susan's Bootcamp	$28.00	$95	$180	$199	First class free
XYZ Fitness	$30.00	N/A	$250	$225	1 week unlimited for $30
HIIT Me Again	$20.00	$85	N/A	$99	Two weeks for $30
Average Package Price	$27.50	$98.25	$212.70	$187	$17.50
Classes Attended per Package	1	5	10	8.5	Unknown
Average Price per Class	$27.50	$19.65	$21.27	$20.77	Unknown

Zooming out to focus on the big picture

Let's say you're a naturally *zoomed-in* person. You are comfortable with numbers and metrics and have been building and analyzing spreadsheets. You need to assess your zoom-out skills.

Zoom-Out Skills Test

Answer these essay questions to test your zoom-out skills:

1. In the wellness field that you are most interested in, list the top two or three most successful businesses in your community.

   _____

   _____

   _____

   _____

2. What qualities do these wellness businesses have in common?

   _____

   _____

   _____

   _____

   _____

3. What qualities differentiate these wellness businesses from each other?

   _____

   _____

   _____

   _____

   _____

4. How have these businesses adapted to the new realities of the post-COVID-19 world?

   _____

   _____

   _____

   _____

5. As a group, why are these wellness businesses more successful than other wellness businesses in your neighborhood of the same type?

   _____

   _____

   _____

   _____

   _____

6. How do the characteristics you outlined in 3 and 4 above reflect the insights you have gained from this book so far?

_____

_____

_____

_____

_____

If you answered these questions easily, without having to spend hours in deep thought or asking others, then you have strong zoom-out thinking skills. You have already translated your enthusiasm for a future in the wellness industry into careful observation of your surroundings and critical thinking about the characteristics of successful wellness businesses. This bodes well for your future!

But if these questions stumped you, or their ambiguity made you uncomfortable, and you did the zoom-in exercise easily, then simply recognize that you are more comfortable with the details and numbers than you are with the big picture. This is not a bad thing, but it is critical to recognize and address your weakness before you conceive and create your wellness business.

It will be imperative to commit to a daily regimen of zoomed-out critical thinking. Start with these questions and then add more of your own. Read everything you can find about wellness trends and visit dozens of other wellness businesses and sample their virtual offerings. While you are receiving their services, rather than simply enjoying the experience, notice the things that distinguish them from others. What's working? What's not? What are the key elements of sight, sound, and smell that define the experience? Is the place busy? Is it clean? Is it well and properly lit? How did the staff make you feel? Were they friendly, courteous, and professional?

Whatever you experience in each wellness business you visit, write down your impressions and take a moment to connect with the fact that none of them happened by accident. Everything you experienced represented something either designed or not designed into the experience.

Talk with Successful Business Owners

If you are a numbers-oriented person, you may have been bothered that there are no "right answers" to the questions in the zoom-out skills test above. They are subjective and that is what makes them so profoundly important. Think about one of your favorite movies or songs. What makes it great? You could cite box office results and album sales, but those numbers only measure greatness; they don't define it. This is because motion pictures and music are experiential, just like wellness classes and services. The most powerful secrets to business success are unlocked by wrestling with the answers to qualitative questions.

How do you unlock those secrets? Through thinking and conversation with people who get it. How do you know they "get it"? By virtue of their own success. Share these questions with anyone who has created a successful business, and I can guarantee you will learn something important. Wellness industry expertise isn't necessary, but business success is.

One of the most powerful insights I gained early in the Mindbody story was from a retired executive from a well-known consumer products company. My wife's parents invited us to a dinner party and were excited for me to meet him. "Oh, you have to meet Lou! He spent a career in business and is really smart!" I looked Lou up online and wasn't optimistic. Lou was old. His career had nothing to do with either software or the wellness industry, and most of his career pre-dated the Internet.

At that point, I had been running Mindbody for several years, had devoted my life to it, and spent nearly every waking moment thinking about it. We had more than 200 employees and thousands of customers all over the world. What could Lou possibly teach me?

The answer was everything.

Before dessert was served, Lou had gained a strong understanding of my business, its opportunities, and its challenges. Even though he had never been to a boutique wellness studio, he quickly came to understand our market opportunity and gave me multiple insights and a transformational perspective that we still draw on today. Thank you, Lou! And thank you in-laws!

Even more important, Lou taught me an important principle: the agile thinking skills of successful business leaders and entrepreneurs are universal.

So, as you look for people to help you zoom in or zoom out, look for evidence of innovation and success, and take note of how many of the five essential traits they possess.

Essential Trait #4: Effective Decision Making

Running any business is dynamic and you will need to make impactful decisions nearly every day. Some of these decisions will have minor impact, like how many of a popular product to reorder or what do with an unhappy customer. Other decisions will have significant impact, such as how to package and price your core services and whether or not to hire someone. Still others could make or break you, such as whether to partner with someone, which technology to use, and where to locate your business.

To make the best decisions you will need to quickly discern important truths, and to do that you will need to think with your head, heart, and gut, all at the same time.

Your Head

Your head represents your conscious mind. You "use your head" to measure things, gather facts, and identify options.

For example, if you are building an indoor cycling studio, your conscious mind can calculate the number of square feet you need to accommodate the class size you want. It can calculate the cost of the bikes needed to create that capacity and would add in the required space for an entrance lobby, front desk, check-in kiosk, bathrooms, changing rooms, etc. Your head would determine where to place your cameras to catch the right live streaming angles for virtual attendees. Then your architect or contractor would check maximum occupancy, fire egress, and ADA (Americans with Disabilities Act) and other code requirements so that you can determine the total square footage of space you need.

But your head cannot tell you *why* you want to run an indoor cycling studio in the first place and how big you ultimately want that business to become. To answer that question, you need to listen to your heart.

Your Heart

Why do you want to run a wellness business and how hard are you willing to work to drive its success? These are questions of the heart. Maybe group exercise changed your life and you want to help others. Maybe you just got screwed over in your corporate job and hate working for others. Maybe you grew up poor and crave financial independence. These are all good reasons, and this is your heart speaking. You'll need to stay tuned into that as you create your plans. But your heart cannot tell you what class size and amenities will create the most addicting client experience. For that you will need your gut.

Your Gut

In decision making, the gut represents your intuition, or what brain scientists would call your subconscious. Whichever you call it, this is where the collective wisdom of your life is stored. It's how you drive a car safely processing thousands of inputs on the road per second, while your head is thinking about something completely different. It's that good or not so good feeling you get about somebody when you first meet them, based on thousands of inputs your head can't possibly keep up with.

Some people would call this bias, and it is, in a sense. When your biases are based on someone's age, gender, heritage, religion, or other factors that have nothing to do with their qualities as a human being, they are bad. But when your biases are informed by thousands of hours of personal experience, they can be immensely helpful in your decision making.

In his landmark book *Blink: The Power of Thinking Without Thinking*, Malcolm Gladwell identified this gut feeling or intuition as residing in our subconscious, where nearly every experience in our lives is recorded. What causes our hand to jerk back when we touch a hot stove? The subconscious. What enables us to see an object shooting out into the road while we are driving and instantly swerve or hit the brakes? Our subconscious.

Coming back to our indoor cycling studio example, you could conduct a double-blind scientific study to determine the optimal size and layout of your classroom. But as a small business owner you probably don't have the time or resources for that. Instead, you need to rely on the short cut of your gut, which will probably get to the right answer quickly, if you've taught or attended hundreds of indoor cycling classes.

I have been to thousands of wellness businesses, and I have a strong bias for clean surfaces, pleasant lighting, and good smells. Even before COVID-19, I didn't need a detailed study to prove that a wellness business would be more successful if it was clean, properly lit, and not smelly. My gut knows that. So too will your gut enable you to evaluate complex questions quickly and effectively.

An Example of Using Your Head, Heart, and Gut

An excellent example of using your head, heart, and gut is how Alexandra Bonetti Perez carefully analyzed multiple New York metropolitan neighborhoods before choosing to open her first Bari Studio location in Tribeca, an excellent decision that proved critical to her early success. She observed:

> *Of course, I researched demographic data—average age, household income, education levels—but the defining difference was the quality of the community. I was looking for a certain vibe, something that you couldn't see in the data. So, I spent a lot of time in the area and just listened and watched. It was when I saw busy professionals—actors, models and executives—waving to each other in the streets that I knew this was the right neighborhood for my studio.*

Alexandra had found the perfect community to match her business vision.

Let's unpack how Alexandra made an excellent decision. First, she tapped into her heart. She developed a passion for exercise after a high-stress consulting career left her feeling depleted and out of shape. Her corporate experiences gave her empathy and compassion for busy professional women and a burning desire to create a wellness business that met their needs.

Next, Alexandra honed her gut instincts. She attended hundreds of classes across dozens of studios and gyms to develop a keen sense of what worked and what didn't. This gave her the key insight that busy professional women hungered for community and needed noticeable results in the least amount of time, and they would be willing to pay a lot for those benefits.

Then Alexandra used her head. Rather than defaulting to a studio location convenient to her home, she obtained demographic data to determine where the highest concentrations of her target audience lived and worked. She then identified multiple candidate neighborhoods in the New York metropolitan area.

Alexandra then leveraged her gut, spending time in each of her candidate neighborhoods before recognizing the clientele and community vibe in Tribeca that matched her insight.

That is how great decisions get made. It's head, heart, and gut all working in concert.

Essential Trait #5: Adaptability

We live in a rapidly changing world. Technology, consumer tastes, and buying habits are evolving constantly and there are few if any business models immune to change. Then every once in a great while something sudden and unexpected like COVID-19 happens that causes a massive shift no one could have anticipated.

A successful business is not a work of art, like Michelangelo's *David*, where its keepers are concerned only with preserving it exactly as the master created it. A successful business is a living and breathing organism, and that organism will either adapt to its changing environment or die.

There are five sure ways to know it's time for your business to adapt:

1. You've been in business more than twelve months and you are still not profitable (see Chapter 8 - Embracing the Holy Grail: Sustained Profitability and Value Creation).
2. The number of new clients coming into your business has trended down in the past year, dipped dramatically in the past ninety days, or fallen off a cliff in the last month.
3. Your retention of existing customers is dropping. Members are cancelling and regulars are attending less often.
4. Your revenue and/or attendance has dropped compared to the same month or quarter of the previous year.
5. Multiple trusted team members or friends are suggesting you make changes.

How do you adapt? Use agile thinking. Get out of your financial reports and outside of your business. Zoom out and look around. What are people favoring today—not just in wellness but in other areas as well? Which businesses are they frequenting and what other experiences are they spending their money on? Investigate new amenities or technologies you can bring into your business to deepen the experience and appeal to your target market client. Or, if your target market client is simply petering out, expand or shift your target and modify your experience to fit that audience. Then zoom back into your business and notice what's going on. Talk to your customers and send out customer satisfaction surveys.

Whatever you do, don't sit at the crossroads too long. A business that is showing declining results is not going to turn around on its own, and it's highly unlikely that you are jumping the gun. By the time you launched your business, you will have a lot of time and treasure invested in your baby. Few people in that scenario want to change it up for no good reason. So, if your head, heart, and gut are telling you it's time to adapt, it's probably long past time to do so.

Enthusiasm, grit, agile thinking, effective decision making, and adaptability are the five essential traits of a successful wellness entrepreneur. That's it. You might be thinking I've missed a few. It's certainly possible, but to be abundantly clear, what follows are some popular beliefs that are absolutely not essential and may even trip you up.

Traits You Don't Need to Be Successful

Being Super Fit

You need to fully understand and be enthusiastic about the industry you are in, and of course you need to take care of yourself and stay well. But successful entrepreneurs also need to keep their lives in balance and remember that there are seven dimensions of wellness. An over-obsession with your own physical fitness may just be vanity, and that could distract you from your business and even be off-putting to your customers. Remember, it's not about you; it's about them. Leave sufficient room in your week to focus on your business, attend to your important relationships, and enjoy some time off. There are only 24 hours in a day.

Getting a College Degree

I recently asked my hair stylist if she dreamed of opening her own salon. She said, "Sure! But I don't want to go back to school." She was surprised to learn that she didn't have to.

Some successful entrepreneurs have impressive academic credentials, but many others never went to college and some didn't finish high school. While there are important professions—engineering, law, and medicine, for example—that require a college degree, the hard truth is that most people pursue courses of study in college that have little or nothing to do with their future careers. Most of what you need to know to build a successful wellness business isn't even taught in school.

My grandfather Neil Stollmeyer didn't finish high school, and he successfully ran a retail business for more than fifty years, a business that thrived across the Great Depression and World War II, providing a comfortable life for him and his family.

But those were simpler times, right? The world is a lot more complex than it was 100 years ago, and a college degree must surely be important to succeed in these times . . . right? The answer is "Yes" for many professions. Few people want to drive over a bridge engineered by somebody who didn't study hard in school, and nobody wants to be wheeled into an operating room to meet a surgeon who didn't go to medical school. But college is not a prerequisite for entrepreneurs.

Josh York is founder and CEO of the at-home personal training franchise GYMGUYZ (www.gymguyz.com). Josh enrolled in college out of high school, because that's what everyone else was doing. Then one day he had an epiphany:

> *I'm in school every day, taking classes in music and calculus. Learning about derivatives and all this crazy stuff, and I started asking myself, 'How am I ever going to use this?' They should have been teaching me about relationships, how to market, how to network, and how to anticipate the challenges and heartaches.*

They should have been teaching me what to do when walls are crashing in and I need to make payroll.

Why don't more schools teach those things? The obvious answer is that people with those experiences are rarely found on college faculties. However, there are many valuable skills you can pick up by selectively taking college courses, particularly in cost effective community colleges.

The first valuable skill you can learn in college is how to organize your ideas and communicate more effectively. But you can also sharpen those skills through the process of identifying what you love, getting certified, and working in the wellness industry.

A second skill you could pick up in college is how to do research and think analytically with numbers, Alexandra Bonetti Perez leveraged her business degree from the University of Pennsylvania's Wharton School to fuel her entrepreneurial success:

I studied Finance and Marketing and learned that I thrive with numbers, KPIs and structure. That enabled me to build a detailed business plan long before I opened my doors at Bari Studios, and gave me clarity as the business developed.

But most entrepreneurs will hire people to do this for them. A business degree is not necessary for business success.

Another relevant skill you could pick up in college is an in-depth understanding of the human body and the science of wellness. My nephew Darik Stollmeyer was a gifted athlete and attended college primarily to play sports. At the same time, he majored in kinesiology and gained a detailed understanding of human anatomy and the mechanics of movement. When Darik later opened his two-location fitness studio Rev SLO (www.revslo .com), his firsthand knowledge of sports performance training and human physiology gave him a powerful foundation for business success. He recounted:

My experience training my body for high-performance sports, combined with the classroom education in anatomy, physiology, and nutrition helped me build a powerful fitness program that works.

But here's the rub: There are few, if any, four-year undergraduate degrees that would materially improve your skills in all three of these areas. A science degree is not likely to improve your communication skills or teach you business. The business degree won't allow you to go deep into human physiology or the science of wellness, and a humanities or social sciences degrees won't teach you either. And either of those paths could cost you 5–6 years and more than $100,000.

Make no mistake, for those who love to learn in a classroom environment, who are passionate about a particular course of study, and who have the means to pay for it without going into debt, college can be a wonderful and empowering experience.

However, if you're over the age of 21 and know that you want to start your own business, then don't focus on college. A few well-chosen community college or online courses related to business or your wellness discipline could be helpful and cost effective, but forget about pursuing a baccalaureate or post-graduate degree. That is somebody else's yardstick and ultimately you won't be measured by it.

7

Five Financial Metrics Every Entrepreneur Must Know

Okay, so you're not going to get a business degree to start your business. And, as we will cover in Chapter 9, you will hire an accountant and book-keeper to manage your accounts and taxes. You don't need to learn accounting to be a successful entrepreneur, but you must understand and watch closely five financial metrics in your business: revenue, cost of revenue, gross profit (or gross margin), operating expenses, and net profit.

Revenue

Revenue is the easiest financial metric to understand and to focus on in your business. **Revenue** is the total sales in your business in a given period of time.

As a first-time business owner, it's thrilling to start earning revenue. Suddenly there are thousands of dollars flowing through your cash register, your website, and your bank account. Imagine after years of planning and months of building, you open the doors of your studio, spa, or salon for the first time with a sales promotion, offering discounts on memberships, services, and products. People are coming in, and they are buying. Wow!

69

Then imagine you look at your bank account at the end of your first week and more than $10,000 has been deposited. It's thrilling. You've made money! You may even tell your friends and worried parents, "I made $10,000 my first week!" Enjoy that dopamine and endorphin hit for a moment. We all need those from time to time.

Now take a deep breath and face the reality that you didn't "make $10,000." Since you were running sale promotions and discounting your products and services, you probably didn't make even half that amount. You may not have made any money at all. That $10,000 may have cost you more than $10,000 to earn. That's why my good friend and highly successful entrepreneur Kevin Comerford says, "Revenue is vanity. Profit is sanity."

Revenue isn't good unless you're earning a profit. Every kid who has ever set up a lemonade stand understands that principle. If a cup of lemonade I'm selling for 25 cents cost me 30 cents to make, then I'm wasting my time. Better to shut down the lemonade stand and go play with my friends. Yet many entrepreneurs forget this basic lemonade stand truth. The next four metrics will help you not make that mistake.

Cost of Revenue

Cost of revenue (also called "cost of sales" or "cost of goods sold") is what it actually cost you directly to earn your revenue, and it is really important. For classes and services, this includes the wages and benefits you paid to the staff who actually taught the classes or delivered the services. For product sales, cost of revenue includes what it cost you to buy the products, including any shipping or import duties you paid to get the products into your business.

To have a wellness business that lasts, your cost of revenue must be less than half of what you collected in revenue for that class, service, or product.

Gross Profit (or Gross Margin)

Gross profit is revenue minus the cost of revenue. This is what you have left after you pay your practitioners and product suppliers, and it is the most important metric in your business. Gross profit is also known as **gross**

margin. Gross profit is usually stated in your local currency, and gross margin is usually stated as a percentage of your revenue. For example, if you buy a single bottle of alkaline mineral water for $1 and sell it for $3, your *revenue* is $3, your *cost of revenue* is $1, your *gross profit* is $3 − $1 = $2, and your *gross margin* is $2 / $3, or 67%.

If you remember nothing else from this section, remember this:

To have a wellness business that lasts, your *gross margin* must be greater than 50% and preferably greater than 60%.

Operating Expenses

Operating expenses are every expense other than your cost of revenue that you must pay in order to keep your business open. This includes marketing expenses, rent, utilities, insurance, software, cleaning, maintenance, repairs, legal and professional expenses, as well as the salaries and benefits of anyone not included in your cost of revenue.

How do you tell the difference between a cost of revenue item and an operating expense? Try this mental exercise: If in a hypothetical world you sold no classes or appointments, and if no one purchased a single product, which expenses would go away that month, and which would still be there? The expenses that go away are your *cost of sales*. The ones you still have to pay are your *operating expenses*, which some old-timers like me call *overhead*.

This single insight will help you structure your business better. Revenue is hard to predict and will ebb and flow with the seasons, right? So the best way to structure a wellness business that lasts is to minimize your operating expenses. Keep your overhead low. That way if you have a terrible sales month, you will minimize how much cash your business consumes that month. Your business will live to fight another day.

Net Profit

Net profit is your actual profit. Also called your "bottom line," this is what you have left after you have paid for all of the expenses of operating your business:

Net Profit = Revenue − Cost of Revenue − Operating Expenses

To have a wellness business that lasts, your net profit should be at least 10% of your revenue.

Examples of Gross Profit, Gross Margin, and Net Profit in Wellness Businesses

Earning Gross Profit from a Fitness Class: You pay an instructor $40 to teach a class of 10 people, and those people paid you a total of $100 for that class. Your customers paid by credit card, so you pay $3 in payment processing fees for that class.

>   Your gross profit on that class is $100 − $40 − $3 = $57.
>   Your gross margin on that class is $57 / $100 = 57%.

Earning Gross Profit from an Appointment: You pay a massage therapist $65 to deliver a massage that your client paid $150 for (before leaving a tip). You paid $3.00 in payment processing fees and $5.00 for laundry and massage oils used in the treatment.

>   Your gross profit on that class is $150 − $65 − $8.00 = $77.
>   Your gross margin on that class is $ 77 / $150 = 51%.

Earning Gross Profit from Retail Products: You sell yoga mats for $39 each, plus sales tax. You order them in bulk from your supplier in boxes of 24 mats for $300 per box. You also pay $50 for shipping (don't forget the shipping!).

>   Your cost per mat sold is ($300 + $50) / 24 = $14.58 each.
>   Your gross profit per mat is $39 − $14.58 = $24.42.
>   Your gross margin on yoga mats is $24.42 / $39 = 63%.

Fitness Studio Example: In the month of January, a high-intensity interval training studio collects $25,000 in memberships, class cards, and drop-ins, and pays their coaches $10,000 to lead classes. They also sell $9,000 in retail products that cost them $4,000 to purchase and ship to the studio. That same month, the studio's bookkeeper records $1,000 in payment processing fees and $14,000 in other operating expenses.

$$\text{Studio Gross Profit} = \text{Gross Profit from Classes} + \text{Gross Profit from}$$

$$\text{Products–Payment Processing Fees}$$

$$= (\$25,000–\$10,000) + (\$9,000–\$4,000)–\$1,000$$

$$= \$15,000 + \$5,000–\$1,000$$

$$= \$19,000$$

$$\text{Studio Net Profit} = \text{Gross Profit–Operating Expenses}$$

$$= \$20,000–\$14,000$$

$$= \$6,000$$

Each month, your bookkeeper will present this information to you in an **income statement**, which is also known as a "profit and loss" statement. This statement should clearly show your revenue, cost of revenue, gross profit, gross margin percentage, operating expenses, and net profit. Your income statement should look something like this:

INCOME STATEMENT, JANUARY 2020

Revenue

Class Sales	$45,000
Product Sales	$ 9,000
Total Revenue	$54,000

Cost of Revenue

Teacher Payroll	$12,000
Cost of Products Sold	$ 4,000
Credit Card Fees	$ 1,500

Total Cost of Revenue	$17,500

Gross Profit	$36,500
Gross Margin Percentage	**68% of Revenue**

Operating Expenses

Desk Staff Wages	$ 5,000
Owner's Salary	$ 7,000
Rent and Utilities	$12,000
Marketing	$ 3,000
Computer Software	$ 1,000
Legal and Accounting	$ 1,000
Other Expenses (e.g, insurance, repairs, cleaning)	$ 1,000

Total Operating Expenses	$30,000

Net Profit	$ 6,500
Net Profit Percentage	**12% of Revenue**

As you can see, this wellness business is healthy. It is earning more than 60% gross margin, it is paying its owner a reasonable base salary, and it is earning a net profit. This is what you must strive for. If your income statement doesn't show you these truths in an easy-to-understand way, have your accountant redo the report so it does. Remember, accountants work for you and your understanding is the most important outcome of their work.

8

Embracing the Holy Grail: Sustained Profitability and Value Creation

Whether you dream of opening a neighborhood store or building a global brand, whether your business will ultimately employ thousands or only yourself, your greatest challenge will be achieving sustained profitability. To those who have never run a business or been a business leader before, the idea of earning profit from your customers may sound banal, trite, and maybe even a little greedy. We are barraged with messages in our culture, literature, movies, and politics suggesting that profitable businesses are bad—that somehow the pursuit of profit is at odds with doing good in the world. That is ridiculous.

In fact, earning a profit in business and doing good in the world are inextricably linked. Any business not generating a reliable and sustainable profit will soon exhaust the bank accounts and will of its owners. That business won't be around long enough to do good for anyone. This is a universal rule of business, and I believe it reflects how the world actually works. Wellness businesses are not exempt from this natural law:

If your business can't pay you, it won't last.

Sustainably profitable wellness businesses are able to consistently deliver a positive net profit (see Chapter 6) after paying their owners the fair market value for the work they are doing in the business. You might have one or two slow months or a month where extraordinary expenses temporarily deplete your bank account or cause you to take on debt. But over time your business should be growing its bank account and paying down its debts.

Drawing a salary from your business may seem like common sense to those who have never started a business. Isn't that the reason you started the business in the first place? Didn't the business owner pass up or leave a good paying job to do this? Drawing a regular salary from your business may seem like common sense, but it is rarely practiced by small business owners. This is because for most entrepreneurs their businesses and their own psyches quickly become linked. Their businesses feel like their children. And, if their child were hungry, no parent would feed themselves first.

But this is not your baby. This is your business, and in business you must feed yourself first for at least two very important reasons.

First, making your business pay you will force you to make the hard decisions that lead to sustained profitability. It will compel you to build at least a 50 percent gross margin into your pricing and to carefully evaluate every expense and every member of your team. It will cause you to work harder and motivate you to dig deeper into all of the topics covered in this book.

Second, by consistently drawing money from your business, you will keep your head, heart, and gut in the game. All of us have experienced falling in love with the wrong person or wrong idea for a time. Our hearts can make mistakes in the near term, but our hearts soon realize the truth. If the relationship isn't feeding our mind, body, and soul, we will soon fall out of love.

Win-lose relationships are simply unsustainable, and the relationship between you and your business if it cannot pay you is win-lose. Your clients are winning from the wellness services you are providing; your staff is winning from the meaningful work and paychecks they are receiving. Even your landlord, vendors, and utility companies are benefiting every time you pay your bills. What about you? After a time, if you don't pay yourself, that sense of being on the short end of a win-lose relationship will inevitably crush your enthusiasm for the business. Your heart will literally not be in it, and when that happens, it's game over.

In addition to the natural law of businesses not lasting without being able to pay their owners, there is a second law of business that wellness entrepreneurs should never forget:

If your business cannot run without you, it will never be worth anything.

If you owned a car that only you could drive, would anybody ever buy it from you? Of course not. Such a car might make an interesting artifact rusting in your front yard, but it would have no value as transportation. The same is true in business.

Regardless of the size of the business you plan to create, I urge you to start with an intention of building something that others will want to buy one day. That is the defining difference between an entrepreneur and someone who is simply self-employed. Being self-employed can be wonderful. Successful self-employed people create meaningful jobs for themselves and enjoy greater independence as a result. This is a laudable goal and might be yours. But when self-employed people stop working, when they are ready to take a sabbatical, join an ashram, or spend a year exploring the world, or if they become seriously injured or ill, their business and income cease. That's because self-employed people are their business.

We see this in our industry with the numerous wellness celebrities who have emerged: teachers, trainers, therapists, and thought leaders who are followed by millions. Many of these people have earned substantial incomes as they built their following and transformed the lives of so many people. But, in far too many cases, the only fuel driving their businesses is themselves—their own special energy, personality, and talent. In other words, the car runs great as long as they are behind the wheel driving, but it won't roll without them. So, I ask you again, will somebody ever buy such a car?

Successful wellness entrepreneurs, on the other hand, create sustainably profitable businesses designed to continue generating a net income for their owners, even after their owners are no longer working. This is called "passive income," one that continues regardless of the effort of its owners. Passive income is what enables a business to continue past the direct involvement of the entrepreneur, and passive income is what makes a business valuable. Sustainably profitable wellness businesses such as these are often sold for three to five times their annual revenue—and much more if they are also growing. Whether you believe your business sale date will come in five years or fifty years, creating it with that end in mind will give you an "exit strategy"—which is essential if you want to attract investors to help you launch or grow it today.

I personally know of fast-growing profitable wellness businesses that have sold for millions of dollars, many times what their entrepreneurs and investors spent creating them. In other words, these wellness businesses have not only created well-paying jobs for their founders and staff, and helped countless people live healthier, happier lives; they have also created real wealth and financial independence for the entrepreneurs who created them. That is the long-term goal I want you to focus on.

Sustained Profitability Is Hard

Here's the rub. Sustainably profitable businesses of any kind are hard to create, and in wellness it is especially true. To be sustainably profitable, a wellness business must do three things really well:

1. Develop a distinctive habit-forming wellness experience that appeals to large numbers of people. We will call this an "addicting experience"—the best possible addiction a person can have (see Chapter 12).
2. Create a value delivery model that reliably reproduces that addicting experience to thousands of people—without the creator present.
3. Earn a high gross margin (see Chapter 7) of at least 50%. This simply means that your clients are willing to pay you at least twice what it cost you to deliver the service to them.

To understand why this is inherently hard, imagine a business that wouldn't be hard, such as selling water in the middle of the desert. Imagine you and I have found a unique opportunity. There is a rest stop halfway between two desert cities, the tap water is terrible, and no one is selling bottled water. We buy a vendor cart and pick up several cases of water that cost 20 cents per bottle. We set up our cart at the rest stop and sell those bottles iced down for $2.00 each. That's a 90% gross margin and still a reasonable price for thirsty travelers. Our first day, commuters, overheated truckers, and harried young parents with red-faced kids line up at our cart. We sell out of inventory before noon. That night we go out to an expensive dinner and toast our fabulous success.

What would happen next in our dream business scenario? People would notice. A lot of people. Before long we'd arrive to see another enterprising duo selling the same water for $1.50, and we immediately start a price war, using sharpies and poster board to advertise our rapidly falling water prices. A couple days later a third vendor shows up, selling flavored drinks, ice cream, and snacks, with a big sign saying, "Ice Cold Bottled Water—25 cents!" They're selling our only product at barely more than we pay for it, to attract customers for other more lucrative products.

We are now forced to shut down our business or engage in vigorous competition, expanding our products, working longer hours in the hot sun, and keeping our prices and gross margins low. Exhausted after a week, we drown our sorrows with a six pack of beer and a store-bought pizza.

This is how the free market works and it is a beautiful thing for consumers. It's why cheap umbrellas show up out of nowhere every time it rains in New York City. It's why the right restaurants are in the right neighborhood, why a cozy coffee shop is around nearly every corner, and why a convenient Uber or Lyft ride is but a phone tap away. The free market puts what we want where we want it and when we want it at a reasonable price.

Sustained Profitability in Wellness

As we discussed in Part I, a Fourth Wave of wellness has kicked off around the globe, fueled by the emergence of hundreds of millions of middle-class or affluent Millennials, advancements in technology, and the accelerating effects of COVID-19. This Fourth Wave will surely disrupt hundreds of thousands of wellness businesses and present huge opportunities for millions more. All of these opportunities will come in an atmosphere of rising consumer expectations, fierce competition, and rapid innovation. To conceive of and plan a sustainably profitable wellness business in that environment, you will need to understand value creation.

Understanding Value Creation

Value creation has a simple economic definition and a much more interesting holistic one. From an economic perspective, value creation describes the actions a person or a team takes to increase the value of a product, a service, or an entire business. To understand the economic definition, let's use the simple example of a bakery.

When a baker combines $10 worth of ingredients and $40 worth of labor and oven time to create a batch of scones that she then sells for $500, that is value creation. The value of the scones she created is ten times greater than what it cost her to make them. To put it in the financial terms we just learned:

> Her *revenue* on thet batch of scones is $500.
> Her *cost of revenue* is $10 + $40 = $50.
> Her *gross profit* is $500 − $50 = $450.
> Her *gross margin* is $450 / $500 = 90%.

That's a good business! If she can sell enough scones and carefully control her overhead and ingredient costs, she can make a good living.

However, when that baker becomes an entrepreneur and decides to turn her bakery into a powerhouse local brand, she will engage in value creation on a whole other level. Suppose she invests $500,000 and five years of effort into her business to create a sustainably profitable business that she then sells to an interested investor for $3 million—that is also value creation.

In the first example, the baker aimed to earn a comfortable living. In the second example, she aimed to create wealth for herself and her family. Both are laudable goals, and it will soon become important for you to decide which goal is yours.

The same principles of value creation apply to wellness businesses that last, except that in our industry there is also a social purpose that creates value for other stakeholders and may transcend the goal of wealth creation for the entrepreneur.

From a big picture point of view, value creation asks whether the business you envision will deliver more value to its stakeholders than it costs in time, money, and effort to create. This is tied to sustained profitability, and depending on how you define "stakeholders" in your business could be about far more than money.

Imagine two founders borrow $300,000 to launch a wellness business, which they operate for ten years and then shut down. If that business earned a profit of exactly $30,000 per year, after paying all its expenses, including fair salaries for the founders and interest on the debt, and the founders used that profit to pay off their debt before they shut down their business and walked away with nothing, an economist or accountant would say that their business created exactly zero value. Yes, you read that right. Zero. Zilch. Nada. But this isn't the full picture, is it?

What if this wellness business also helped thousands of people in its community live healthier, happier lives and created a decade's worth of good jobs for dozens of wellness practitioners and staff?

What if that business helped catalyze a revitalization of its neighborhood, causing dozens of other useful small businesses to sprout up?

What if the ten-year run of that business improved the lives of its founders, enabling them to earn a good living and vastly increase their business skills doing something they loved?

What if that business gave its founders flexibility, enabling them to spend more time with their young children before they left home?

Lastly, what if that business gave its founders a greater sense of purpose and helped them achieve high esteem and self-actualization on Maslow's hierarchy of needs?

If any of those things were true, then we could say that those founders engaged in value creation, even if they were unable to create an economic profit or wealth for their family.

As a wellness entrepreneur, the key principle to remember when you are thinking about value creation is that "value" is in the eyes of the beholder. Every stakeholder of the business—its founder, owners, staff, customers, and community—will define the value they received from that business in their own terms.

Therefore, whether you are planning life as a self employed independent wellness professional or the leader of a substantial team, it is imperative that you first define the value you want to yield from your business. Write down the first things that come to your mind when you read these questions:

1. In my personal life, I want my wellness business to give me

   _____

   _____

   _____

2. In my professional life, I want my wellness business to give me

   _____

   _____

   _____

3. In the first year after my wellness business starts, I need a steady income of at least $_____ per month.

4. When my wellness business is fully successful, I expect to earn at least $_____ per year.

5. After I shut down or sell my business, and pay off all business-related debts, I want to walk away with $_____.

6. During the course of its operational life, I want my wellness business to create these values for our other stakeholders:

   Our Clients:

   _____

   _____

   _____

   Our Staff:

   _____

   _____

   _____

   Our Neighborhood:

   _____

   _____

   _____

   Others:

   _____

   _____

   _____

If you have one or more planned business partners, ask each of them to write down their responses to the same questions, and then share them with each other. These responses will form the basis of your business value creation vision. You will refer back to these when you craft your business plan and partnership agreements.

PART III

Conceive Your Business

9

Select Your Mentor, Lawyer, and Accountant

The Importance of a Mentor

Mentors are people who volunteer their time and energy to help you think through the vision, plan, launch, and operation of your business. They can act as an active coach with a regular plan of structured meetings with you or simply as a sounding board available to listen when you need them. Your first business mentor may be an early investor who stands to profit from your success, but the principal motivation in mentoring you should be more altruistic than personal gain. Ideal mentors are people with decades of business experience who recognize how many people have helped them along their journey. They are willing to spend time with you because they enjoy helping others and want to "pay it forward."

Mentors should not be directly paid for their efforts. If someone approaches you with such a "mentor for hire" proposition, politely decline. That kind of relationship is called business coaching or consulting, and while there are a few such coaches out there who are very good, most will not be worth the cost at this stage. The wisdom and knowledge you will need to conceive a successful wellness business will be largely unique to this industry, and I have strived to include all of it in this book.

Most important, mentors with the wisdom and knowledge to start and run a successful business have achieved sufficient financial success that they don't need to charge you for their time. An already wealthy person who would charge an aspiring entrepreneur for their advice is not the kind of mentor you need. Realizing your vision will probably cost far more than you are imagining at this stage, so conserve your cash! You may decide to hire a consultant or business coach as you are launching your business, but now is not the time.

Qualities to Look For

The most important consideration when choosing mentors is that you and they have a natural rapport, and they are genuinely interested in your success. You actually enjoy spending time together, talking about your business plans, challenges, and life in general. I personally believe the hallmark of successful entrepreneurs is how deeply they have integrated their own personal and professional lives. In every case I have seen, successful entrepreneurs' business is inextricably woven into their life. It is their vocation, their passion, their hobby, and their main source of wealth. The hallmark of such people is how seamlessly their conversation flows from business to personal.

The next most important quality of good mentors is intellectual curiosity. Through many years of direct business experience, they have accumulated a great deal of knowledge. Their basic approach to life is more learner than knower. Good mentors are fascinated by your plans. They ask insightful questions and genuinely listen to your responses. From these dialogs they learn who you are deep down. They learn about your natural gifts and the fire in your belly driving you to start yours business. They also learn about your gaps, where you need to develop further to become a successful entrepreneur. These insights will make them invaluable as your entrepreneurial journey develops.

Examples of Great Mentors

How do I know so much about good mentors? Because I have been blessed with several great mentors in my life. First and foremost of these has been my dad, Jerry Stollmeyer, who successfully ran his own retail business for thirty years and began mentoring me about business long before Blake Beltram and I launched Mindbody. Throughout my two-decade journey of leading Mindbody from a tiny startup in my garage to the global business it is today, my dad has been my sounding board and confidant. His innate curiosity and profound wisdom have fueled my endurance and helped me think through innumerable challenges.

As I think back on hundreds of conversations, I realize that my dad has spent more time listening than talking. When he did speak, his words truly mattered—the timely insight, the keen observation, or the thought-provoking question. His words carried weight for me not just because he is my dad and has been there my whole life. More important to the topic for mentorship, my dad took the time to truly know me as an adult and an entrepreneur. This gave him the ability to see and reinforce the best of my best qualities and to gently correct my worst. These are the hallmarks of a great business mentor, and being born with one as a father is one of the greatest gifts in my life.

Another great mentor example is Stender Sweeney, a leader in the Pasadena Angels group and one of Mindbody's first investors outside of friends and family. Stender had a long career as a highly successful corporate senior executive and public company board director before becoming a leader in the southern California angel investor scene. My introduction to Stender in 2004 came at a pivotal moment in Mindbody history. We had outgrown our original desktop software and were in the process of developing Mindbody Online, a breakthrough cloud version of our product. Accessing software via a web browser or mobile app is the norm today, but in 2004 only a few other software companies in the world had attempted to create it, and the process was rife with challenges. On top of this, to abandon the desktop software we had spent years building for something completely new was expensive, and we had very little cash.

I consider the fact that Stender Sweeney entered my life while we were making that critical decision as divine intervention. Stender not only evaluated and then endorsed me and Mindbody as promising investments for dozens of other angel investors, he became my personal mentor helping me navigate multiple crucial decisions, including our migration to the cloud. In September 2005, we successfully raised our first financing outside of friends and family, a "Series A" financing round of $1.1 million from a consortium of Pasadena Angels and Tech Coast Angels investors. That would not have happened without Stender. But his help went far beyond securing money.

Over the next decade, across hundreds of phone calls and dozens of face-to-face meetings, Stender mentored me through the challenges of scaling a business from my garage to a global company. He also served on Mindbody's board of directors and coached me numerous times on how to manage relationships with our other investors and board members. Yes, one could say that Stender was protecting his investment, but the simple truth is the value of the time he gave me and Mindbody vastly exceeded the dollars he invested. In the end, Stender's investment in Mindbody did very well for him and the rest of the Sweeney family, but that outcome was highly unlikely in the early years of our relationship, when he volunteered his time to mentor me free of charge.

Finding Your Mentor

How do you find mentors like my dad and Stender? It's not easy, because truly wise and accomplished people who won't demand something in return are rare, and there are many other entrepreneurs who would like time with them as well. This may sound a little strange, but treat your search for an effective mentor in the same way you would approach the search for a life partner. Specifically:

1. Decide first the characteristics you are looking for. Which experiences and personal qualities matter most to you? I have listed several that mattered most to me above, but your list may be different.
2. Get outside of your own social circle and generational group. You are looking for someone with life experience, so become involved in local

business and civic groups like the Chamber of Commerce or Rotary Club.

3. Let people know that you are developing your own business plan. There is no reason to keep that fact a tightly held secret.

4. Be interesting by being interested. Listen more than you talk, and truly absorb what others are saying, rather than trying to simply promote your own agenda. Nothing is more off-putting than somebody who only talks about themselves.

5. Don't try to force it. Look for the signals that somebody is truly interested in your success before making the ask.

Your search for a good mentor may take years. Meanwhile, you have mountains to climb and a business to create, so proceed with the far easier task of engaging with a good business lawyer and certified public accountant (CPA).

The Importance of Lawyers, Accountants, and Bookkeepers

Most people and many small business owners have negative opinions of lawyers and ambivalent feelings about accountants. This is because most people aren't usually talking to a lawyer unless there is a serious problem, and accountants are more often than not the bearers of bad news—such as the taxes that are due or the deductions you can't take. These are corrective actions and you will be successful and save a lot of money and pain by being proactive. Make no mistake, these professionals are essential to an entrepreneur, and the really good ones are invaluable.

As a wellness entrepreneur, you will need to think of your lawyer and accountant as you do your dentist. You will either spend a small amount for regular proactive care now, or you will be in for a painful and expensive root canal later. The reason so many businesspeople have negative attitudes about lawyers is because they didn't take a proactive approach. Their first interaction with a lawyer or CPA is in the midst of a legal crisis, which is a bit like going to the dentist for the first time with a mouthful of cavities and advanced gum disease. At that point, it's going to hurt and bills will be brutal.

Why You Need to Engage a Good Lawyer Early

The most important work of your business attorney is done before your business starts. It is in the planning stages that your lawyer will come to understand your business vision, explain important legal and regulatory requirements, explain your options for legal entity, and help you select the one that best suits your personal needs. Your lawyer will also review and help draft the critical early agreements you will need to execute before you start your business—most important, your business partnership and investor agreements, if you have those.

Even if you are simply starting out as an independent teacher, trainer, or therapist, there will be liability releases and independent contractor agreements to execute. Never sign an agreement without having a lawyer review it. Even if you don't think you are in a position to negotiate, your lawyer can at least help you advise you of any concerns. In professional life, there is no such thing as a "standard agreement," and you may be able to negotiate better terms.

If you are creating a brick-and-mortar studio, spa, or salon, there will be important agreements with your employees and other service providers, a commercial lease to negotiate, and a general contractor to engage for tenant improvements.

If you are creating a digital wellness business, there will be agreements to execute with software and web developers, hosting agreements to negotiate, and consumer privacy laws and other regulations to adhere to. Your lawyer should definitely be involved in these long before you are lining up these critical business relationships.

If you are co-creating your business with a partner or investor, your agreements with those individuals need to clearly spell out the nature of your relationship. Key questions your partnership agreements must answer include:

1. How much capital is each partner contributing and how much ownership will they receive in the business?
2. If one or more partners is contributing "sweat equity" (their work and their ideas create their ownership), what period of time do they need to contribute before that ownership is real?

3. What roles will the partners fill in the business, and who is in charge?
4. If the partners are co-equal, how will important decisions get made?
5. How much effort is each partner required to contribute to the business to maintain their ownership or leadership status in the business, and what happens if a partner decides to leave the business because they fell in love with someone in Costa Rica or have decided to join an ashram?
6. If all the partners agree to shut down the business, how will the remaining assets and liabilities of the business be distributed?

Just reading this list should convince you of my point: you need a good lawyer!

Selecting Your Lawyer

To find a great lawyer, first talk to your mentor, if you have one, and with other small business owners in your community. Get multiple referrals and ask the referrers for details on their experience with that attorney. Were they helpful and proactive? Did they give good advice? Did they make any mistakes? Were their bills reasonable?

Then select your top three finalists and interview each of them. This "first consultation" should be free, and if any lawyer resists that, then cross them off your list. When you do meet with your final candidates, explain your business plans and see if they ask the right questions (such as those above). Listen to your head, heart, and gut when you are with them. Does this lawyer have relevant small business experience? How do they make you feel when you are with them? Are they condescending or supportive? Are they reactive or calming? Do they present problems or do they offer solutions? Do they project fear or quiet confidence? Are they supportive of your business plans or skeptical?

Your lawyer should be capable and honest and pleasant to be around. They should be skilled at uncovering important facts about you and your business and willing to confront you with those facts in an honest and productive way. They should treat you as the client you are, with fundamental respect and a manner that builds your confidence and helps you feel good. Life is too short to work with jerks. Remember, in the attorney-client relationship you are in control.

Accounting Professionals Are Worth Every Dime

You will need two types of accounting professionals to help you manage your business: a certified public accountant (CPA) and a bookkeeper. You'll need the CPA early in your planning process, and you'll need to hire a bookkeeper about a month or two before you launch.

Understanding Why You Need a CPA

A CPA is a highly trained professional with an undergraduate degree in finance or accounting, multiple years of experience, and a state license to practice accounting. CPAs adhere to a strict professional code that includes continuing education to remain current in constantly changing tax laws. In addition, they are qualified to act as your "fiduciary," which means they are required to act solely in your best interest and can represent you in dealings with tax authorities.

Because the standards of the CPA licensing process are so demanding, these highly qualified professionals are expensive, typically charging $200–$300 per hour or more in major metropolitan areas. But their services are essential, particularly at the formation of your business and later when you file quarterly and annual tax returns.

You should select your CPA shortly after engaging your attorney, who will likely make recommendations. Don't automatically take your attorney's recommendation. Get additional referrals from mentors and small business owners in your community. Conduct the same vigorous reference check and interview process that you used to select your attorney. Then make your best decision leveraging your head, your heart, and your gut. This takes time, but it is oh so worth it.

Your accountant and attorney will then collaborate to ensure that your business entity is optimally structured to align with your personal financial situation and to legally minimize future taxes. Once your business is up and running, they will help you plan and execute on your tax payments and tax returns. Finally, your accountant will help you select the second accounting professional you will need—your bookkeeper.

Knowing What a Bookkeeper Can Do for You

A bookkeeper is typically someone who lacks a formal accounting education but has broad business experience helping entrepreneurs track their financial results, process payroll, collect from people who owe you money ("accounts receivable"), and pay bills ("accounts payable"). Even if you love bookkeeping, and perhaps even did that work in your prior career, I strongly urge you to outsource this activity to someone else as soon as possible. For a few hundred dollars per month, a competent bookkeeper will handle the details and ensure that you are kept in touch with the financial truths of your business. They will give you the time to zoom in on other aspects of your business you cannot so easily delegate—such as building your team, marketing, and delivering exceptional experiences to your clients—and zoom out to always keep the big picture in mind.

Selecting Your Accounting Professionals

Thanks to cloud software, neither your accountant nor your bookkeeper have to be physically present in your business, or even live nearby. They can access your sales and payroll information, as well as your online accounting software, from anywhere in the world. And thanks to the rapid growth of the wellness industry, there are hundreds of highly skilled CPAs and thousands of affordable bookkeepers directly experienced with small wellness businesses. Be sure your CPA is licensed in your state and your bookkeeper is experienced there, but other than that it doesn't matter where either of them live.

Hiring a Business Coach or Consultant

If you are starting as an independent wellness professional, you don't need a business coach. But if you are planning a more substantial brick-and-mortar or virtual wellness business and have the budget for a coach, engaging one could be extremely helpful. If you do, be aware that there are no universal standards or requirements to become a business consultant. Many are highly experienced and skilled in wellness businesses, but many others have little relevant experience, and their advice could prove distracting or even harmful. Your selection process should be similar to the one outlined for your attorney and CPA, with the addition of leveraging wellness industry contacts and resources.

At Mindbody, we have a Certified Consultant program that carefully vets people for their wellness industry experience, expertise, and reputation. We offer this consultant certification program as a free service to the wellness industry and collect no fees from the consultants hired from our website (see https://marketplace.mindbodyonline.com/consultants). We encourage you to peruse the list and speak with those who might be a good fit for you.

10 | Define Your Target Market

Clients are the most important element of any business. Without clients you don't have a business at all. Many wellness businesses prefer to give their clients different labels, such as "members," "students," or "athletes," and you may have good reason to do that. Make no mistake: no matter what you call them, they are still your clients, and your clients are your customers. These are people who, of their own free will, have agreed to pay you their hard-earned money for a wellness benefit you are promising to bestow on them. Your clients are the people your business and you are here to serve.

This way of thinking is important because it puts you into the mindset of a servant leader, rather than of the "master" or "guru," which pervades many wellness disciplines. Regardless of how that humble mindset may make you feel in the moment, I promise it will make you far more effective and successful as a business owner. I have never met a sustainably successful entrepreneur who is arrogant. In fact, for those who achieve early success and fall into the arrogance trap, it is commonly their hubris that later degrades their business and brings them down.

One of the common mistakes aspiring entrepreneurs make is thinking too broadly about the clients they want to serve. Defining a very large group of people as your target clients seems to make intuitive sense. If you position your business to address the need of the largest number of people, then you need to attract only a small fraction of those to achieve a sustainable business. On the surface, such a strategy would seem to increase your probability of success. But in reality the opposite is true. When you position your business to serve too broad an audience, you end up trying to be everything to everybody—and pleasing no one.

In our modern world of continuous innovation, products and services that seemed "good enough" a few years ago are no longer desirable. We live in an amazing time where billions of people are in pursuit of the higher levels of Maslow's hierarchy of needs, and the competitive marketplace has responded with a dazzling array of extremely well-designed products and experiences that cater precisely to our tastes—from the kinds of meals we eat, to the places we go to socialize, to the vacations we take and the clothes we buy. And the boutique wellness industry is no exception. An industry that began in the Second Wave of the late 1990s with only a few different business types has evolved into hundreds of specialized business types today.

Therefore, whether you are conceiving a small wellness business designed to address the needs of a few hundred people in your community or the global wellness brand targeting millions of consumers worldwide, the only way to draw clients to your business, get them talking about you, and keep them coming back is by carefully crafting habit-forming experiences that appeal to their needs, desires, and tastes. You cannot do that without precisely defining your target market and knowing those clients as deeply as possible.

Wellness entrepreneurs who do this well turn their clients into devoted loyalists—people who form a community around your business, attend whenever they can, and spontaneously invite close friends and family to join the "tribe." This kind of client loyalty sets off a virtuous cycle of growth and profitability that will keep you energized and help you attract and retain the best wellness professionals and staff to your team. Everyone wants to join a winning team!

That beautiful dynamic is set into motion when you do the work to carefully define your target market clients, deeply understand their needs, and design a differentiated wellness experience that they will love.

Defining a Target Market Is Not an Excuse to Discriminate

This is a good time to point out something I hope is obvious. Your target market should never be defined in terms of race, ethnicity, nationality, appearance, gender, or sexual orientation. Doing so is discriminatory and wrong. And it's ineffective. People moving up Maslow's hierarchy of needs today, the people you want to attract to your business, are not inspired by outdated modes of thinking.

Target markets today are defined by the personalities, motivations, and needs of the people who typify that market. You will identify your target market clients by their tastes, preferences, life choices, and willingness to invest time and money into your type of wellness experience. As wellness practitioners and entrepreneurs, you must identify these target markets to create businesses that prosper and last. At the same time, your commitment to wellness calls you to ensure your business is welcoming to people from all walks of life. People you never expect may walk through your doors or engage with you online, and your first job as practitioners and entrepreneurs is to welcome them.

Defining the Right Target Market

To successfully define your ideal target market clients, design experiences they will enjoy, and attract them to your business, it is essential that you know them well and that you love them. If you don't know them well, it will be impossible to create experiences they most desire. If you don't love them, you will soon grow very tired of serving them.

Your target market clients must define a group large enough to fuel the thriving business you are envisioning and distinct enough to focus on. In some cases, it may be appropriate to define two complementary client types. If you live in a hip college town, "young professionals and college students" probably describes two groups of people who already socialize together and are likely to have similar preferences. The same may be true for "Millennial professionals and stay-at-home parents," or "athletes and outdoor enthusiasts," or "social progressives and the environmentally conscious."

Trying to focus concurrently on two or more highly disparate groups because they happen to live or work near your business, such as "value-seeking college students and high-income professionals" will diffuse your focus and confuse your brand. Most important, this split focus will prevent you from designing experiences that fully satisfy either group. It is also important to consider the disposable income and philosophies of your target market group.

Thinking about the people you most want to serve with your wellness business, record the first responses that come to your mind when you read these questions:

1. What kinds of clients will enable me to most easily achieve my wellness business purpose? (Be specific about gender, age, work status, location, affinity, personality, and income class.) *We will call these your target market clients.*

   _____

   _____

   _____

2. What kinds of wellness activities do my target market clients engage with today?

   _____

   _____

   _____

3. What is the typical annual household income of my target market clients?

   _____

4. What other kinds of experiences do my target market clients currently spend their money on (shopping, dining, bars, coffee shops, entertainment, vacations, etc.)?

   _____

   _____

   _____

   _____

   _____

5. How much do I believe my target market clients would be willing to spend each month on the wellness products and services I am planning to offer?

   _____

6. How many engaged target market clients will I need to generate the following monthly revenue in my business:

$10,000: _____

$25,000: _____

$50,000: _____

$75,000: _____

$100,000: _____

Sizing Your Target Market

How many potential clients do you need in your target market? That depends on the price point of your services and the likely purchasing frequency of members or loyal clients. You'll want to do the math, conservatively estimating how much revenue you can earn from each. For now, here are some good rules of thumb on the numbers of target market clients most wellness businesses need to last:

- For an independent wellness professional: a target market of at least 2,000 potential clients in your service area yielding a foundation of at least 100 regular clients
- For a retail boutique wellness business: a target market of at least 10,000 potential clients within commuting distance from your business (This gives you the opportunity to generate a stable target client base of at least 200 auto-pay memberships.)
- For a virtual wellness business: a target global market of several million people so that a steady conversion of a tiny fraction of those people over time will gradually build into a base of high-gross-margin recurring revenue

With that in mind, take a look at your answers above and try again. In one sentence, define your target market client:

_____

Your target market client should be in focus now. Based upon your answers to questions 5 and 6 above, and the decisions you will make in the next chapter, you will soon find out if you can earn a good living building a wellness business that lasts.

11

Evaluate Retail versus Home–Based and Virtual Business Options

Today, thanks to rapid advances in cloud software, virtual delivery platforms, and connected devices, and thanks to the catalyzing impact of COVID-19 on our industry, there are more choices than ever when deciding how to deliver wellness as an independent practitioner or entrepreneur. These value delivery options can be placed in one of six classes:

Class I: Home-based wellness delivery, where you meet your clients in your or their homes

Class II: Third-party wellness delivery, where you meet your clients face-to-face in their workplace (as part of corporate wellness) or in a short-term sublet space

Class III: Virtual wellness delivery, where you leverage on-demand or streaming technologies to deliver experiences to clientele anywhere in the world

Class IV: Retail wellness delivery, where you execute a long-term lease and perform tenant improvements to a classic brick-and-mortar location that carries your business name on the door

Class V: Hybrid wellness delivery, where you incorporate two or more (and perhaps all four) of the above models to reach your customers
Class VI: Multi-location wellness delivery with owner-operated or franchise models

Understanding the Options

We can think of these options as Class I–VI white-water rapids, because that is an apt metaphor. Just as with white-water rafting, the potential risk of a Class I or II wellness business is minor, but it's not very exciting either. A Class I or II wellness business can be relaxing and fun, and if it doesn't work out, you may only lose a few thousand dollars and some time.

As you move up to Class III, virtual wellness delivery, the excitement level grows, along with the required level of investment and potential losses. This may seem surprising to some. Anyone can set up a YouTube channel, Facebook, or Instagram page for free and begin uploading videos in under a day. Similarly, COVID-19 taught us all that anyone can livestream a wellness experience through Zoom, Facebook, or Instagram for little or no cost. The barriers to entry and ease of setup are low for virtual wellness delivery, and that is precisely the problem for any serious entrepreneur.

There are tens of millions of YouTube Channels, and nearly one million hours of new video content is being uploaded *each day*. Attracting viewers in the middle of that flood of free content is a bit like walking down New York's 5th Avenue during rush hour with a stack of leaflets in your hand and hoping that people will spontaneously start taking them from you.

To make matters worse, it is really hard to make money that way. YouTube has a program called AdSense where they pay you to place third-party ads on your YouTube Channel, but you need to have at least 1,000 subscribers and 4,000 hours of subscriber watch time in a trailing twelve-month period to qualify for the program. You will need at least a thousand times that activity to make even a meager income off of it.

You can learn everything you need to know about AdSense by searching on Google, but suffice it to say, unless you already have a huge following, your path to earning a living from AdSense as a wellness entrepreneur is essentially impossible. If you try to do it by paying for your own advertising, you could burn through tens of thousands of dollars before making your first dollar back.

The only effective way for most wellness practitioners and entrepreneurs to make a living off of virtual wellness delivery is to restrict access to your on-demand and streaming video content behind a paywall. That means that only the paying clients you authorize can access it. Until recently, this has been out of reach for most wellness business owners.

Fortunately, virtual class and appointment delivery platforms have advanced rapidly in recent years, and COVID-19 acted as a huge accelerant. Mindbody's own Virtual Wellness Platform integrates with our business management solutions, enabling wellness practitioners or entrepreneurs to easily add online virtual offerings to their offline face-to-face experiences. The Virtual Wellness Platform then enables you to market your virtual content through the Mindbody app.

In this manner you can create relationships with local clientele through Class I or Class II delivery models and then extend your reach and engagement through on-demand and streaming methods. This hybrid approach combines the lower risk and cost advantages of a Class I or II delivery model with the digital extension of Class III, long before you consider taking the leap to Class IV.

Classes IV, V, and VI delivery models, which require your own brick-and-mortar locations, are by far the most expensive and risky routes. The startup cost for a single boutique brick-and-mortar wellness location can range anywhere from $250,000 to $500,000. But if you have prepared yourself for the journey and follow the guidelines of Parts III and IV, your odds of creating a wellness business that lasts are quite good.

My Wife's Journey through the Rapids

With several years' experience serving Class IV, V, and VI businesses at Mindbody, my wife, Jill, had seen these entrepreneurial stories play out hundreds of times. Armed with those experiences and her prior career as a marketing consultant, she decided to leave Mindbody in 2011 to embark on her own Hero's Journey as a wellness entrepreneur.

Jill's first step was to attend an area massage school and obtain her license as a Certified Massage Therapist (CMT). In 2012 she launched her Class I wellness business, setting up a treatment room in our home and offering massages to friends and family. Soon, those friends and family started referring others and her at-home massage business grew.

A year later, Jill made the leap to a Class II delivery model, subletting a treatment room in a local spa and splitting the monthly rent with another therapist friend. She and her friend further agreed to share a subscription to Mindbody's business management platform to manage their schedules, take online bookings, and process credit card payments. While gradually ramping up her low-overhead, independent massage business, she was working on her real business plan.

In 2014, we signed a five-year lease on a 4,000-square-foot retail space in our local downtown. We hired a lawyer and accountant to set up our LLC, a consultant to help her create a business plan, and an architect and contractor to design and build out a truly exceptional spa and wellness center. East Wellbeing and Tea Spa was beautiful. It had two single and one couples massage rooms, each with soaking tubs, as well as two acupuncture/facial rooms, a meditation/yoga room, and a retail/tea service area. All in, we spent over $400,000 on tenant improvements and business setup before Jill opened her doors in September 2015.

There were three main benefits of Jill's phased approach through Classes I and II:

1. It gave her time to gain firsthand industry experience while earning a moderate income and minimizing out-of-pocket expenses.
2. It gave us time to build enough savings to pay for the business startup costs without going into debt.
3. Her time as an independent practitioner gave her four glorious years of schedule flexibility. This enabled her to spend more time with our four kids while they were all still at home and gave us more time together. Those were irreplaceable years and neither of us have ever regretted the decision.

Learn from Our Mistakes

But hindsight is 20:20, and looking back on it now, we skipped several steps outlined in Chapter 5. Did you spot them?

First, while Jill got her massage certification and began working directly with clients, she never gained experience managing an established spa. In retrospect, with her experience in business and massage therapy, she would have been a highly desirable spa manager and probably could have negotiated good compensation and a flexible as she gained important small business management experience.

Second, Jill didn't have access to the information in Parts I and II of this book: to truly prepare herself for the journey, to test her ideas, and to build sustained profitability and value creation into her business model. We knew many of these concepts ten years ago but hadn't crystalized them into a coherent narrative yet.

A Hard Decision

As you may be guessing by now, our wellness business didn't last. In early 2020, while I was midway through writing this book, Jill and I had a heart-to-heart conversation and decided not to renew our lease. We planned to sell the business before the end of the year.

Then COVID-19 hit and accelerated our plans. After several weeks of COVID forced shutdown, with an unclear understanding of when our business would be able to reopen, Jill called a staff meeting via Zoom and let her team know we were closing the business for good.

This was an incredibly difficult decision for both of us, but it was gut-wrenching for Jill. She had poured her heart and soul into her business and her team. The space was inspired and uniquely beautiful. Her loyal clients and staff loved it, and she loved them.

But the business was adding more stress in our life, and in the end, our decision came down to the hard reality that after nearly five years it was still not sustainably profitable. Thinking through the additional hard work and dollars we would need to invest to get it there, we both realized that we didn't want it badly enough. We no longer needed a second income and other priorities in our life had become more important. That's how most wellness businesses end: when its owners no longer possess the will or the capital to continue the Hero's Journey.

Yes, it hurts to lose most of the $400,000 we invested into that business. But we are extremely fortunate that we could afford to absorb the loss. If we had a more typical household income and net worth and had gone into debt to launch our wellness business, it could have been a severe financial setback.

What's the one thing we wish we had known five years ago? That's the subject of the next chapter.

12

Lay Your Foundation with Your Competitive Advantage

To create a wellness business that lasts, you need to build **competitive advantage** into your plan. This means that your business has one of the following:

A cost advantage. It costs your wellness business less than your competitors to deliver a wellness experience that is equivalently valued by your target market clients.

An experience advantage. Your wellness business is able to deliver a differentiated experience that your target market clients place more value on and will pay more for.

The most successful wellness businesses have both.

Understanding Cost Advantage

A competitive cost advantage means that your business spends less delivering a wellness experience to each client than your competition does.

Consider two yoga studios directly competing for the same clients on the same city block in some downtown shopping core. Both owners have

107

designed their class experience to appeal to the same type of target market clients. Studio North is the smaller of the two. It can comfortably accommodate no more than 15 people in a class and averages 8 people per class in a typical week. Meanwhile, Studio South across the street is physically larger. It can accommodate up to 30 people and averages 16 people per class.

To keep the math simple, let's assume both studios pay their yoga teachers $40 per class and have similar rent and operating expenses.

On average, Studio North is paying its teachers:

$40 per class/8 people per class = $5 per class attendee

Thanks to its larger studio size and higher average attendance, Studio South is paying its teachers:

$40 per class/16 people per class = $2.50 per class attendee

Studio South has a $2.50 per client competitive cost advantage over Studio North. This gives its owners three beneficial options:

1. Studio South could choose to keep its prices the same as Studio North and quietly pocket the extra profit.
2. Studio South could choose to invest its extra profit into more technology-driven marketing and promotion, increasing the average number of clients in each class and further extending its competitive cost advantage.
3. Studio South could choose to invest its additional profits into improving its client experience, differentiating it from Studio North and drawing even more clients in the door. It might remodel the studio, add dressing rooms, showers, childcare, or other amenities that its target market clients desire. It might give out free tea or smoothies after each class and still keep its per client cost in each class lower than Studio North's.

Now imagine if Studio South did a combination of all of the above. Its average class attendance, revenue, and profits would soar.

A competitive cost advantage is a powerful thing in business, and you should strive to design cost advantage into your business plan from day one.

You can do this by controlling costs that don't directly improve the experiences of your clients, rooting out time-wasting steps that reduce the number of clients you can serve in a day, and maximizing your capacity utilization.

Value Creation and Pricing

To understand how to price something, you will first want to understand the prices for the same or similar services in your neighborhood. The spreadsheet you built for the zoom-in exercise in Chapter 6 is a good start—but it's just a start. You need to go deeper on this.

To optimally price your products and services, you will need to understand the close connection between experience and value. The first reflex of every entrepreneur is to underprice your competition. It's a natural thing to do. Your business is unknown and you're trying to get known. But you will create a far better and more sustainable business if you instead design your experiences in a way that your target market clients will ascribe a higher value to them, and then charge for that value.

Think about these examples from your daily life:

- Why are we willing to pay far more for any meal cooked by others than for that same food cooked at home?
- When we go out to eat, why are we willing to pay more for the same food served in a nice dining room with cloth napkins and attentive staff?
- When we go to the movies, why will we pay more for reclining seats with a better view?
- How are airlines able to charge more for a plane ticket purchased at the last minute than one purchased months in advance?
- Why do hotel and event prices usually move in the opposite direction, with prices usually cheaper when purchased at the last minute?

The answers to these questions reveal the direct link between experience delivery, value creation, and price. Let's focus first for a moment on the time-bound price questions.

How are airlines able to charge more for a plane ticket purchased at the last minute than one purchased months in advance? Because purchasing airline tickets last minute implies urgency and appeals to a different customer.

Usually the passenger is a business traveler with an important and valuable reason to be in Dallas tomorrow. Airlines have become increasingly adept at matching their flight schedules to expected demand, so last-minute tickets are scarce. That seat has more value to the last-minute traveler than to the one who booked it months ago.

Why do hotel and event prices usually move in the opposite direction, with prices usually cheaper when purchased at the last minute? Because the capacity of hotels and event centers is fixed. They cannot add or subtract seats to meet changing demand; for most games and events, the seats are undersold. As it costs them little or nothing for the venue to bring in more people (in fact, they will make more in food and drink sales), any price received for that last-minute ticket sale is found money.

That dynamic closely matches class-based wellness businesses, where the capacity of the business is fixed and sized for peak demand, and the cost of filling the last remaining spots is approximately zero. It's different in appointment-based services, where the cost of the practitioner increases for every additional service sold. Still, if you could sell that additional hour for a few dollars more than it cost you to deliver it, you've still created value, right? Maybe.

You've created value if the act of offering that class or service for less does not "cannibalize" regular full-price-paying customers. Cannibalization occurs when the discounted sale "eats" the full-priced sale, meaning a normally full-price paying customer converts into a discounted purchase. This is why your discounts and promotions need to be carefully targeted.

Value Creation and Discounting

To prevent cannibalization, a discount or promotion needs to be either attached to a limited set of offerings perceived as lower value by your customers or reserved for a different class of customer who would not normally pay full price.

There are four common examples of effective discounting in the wellness industry:

1. **Introductory offers.** These offers are limited to first-time customers only and therefore cannot cannibalize your full-price-paying customers.

2. **Reengagement offers.** These offers are sent specifically to customers who have not returned to the business for several weeks or months. Example:
   - A "We miss you" email or text that offers a discounted return purchase (e.g., "Book now and we'll give you half off your first session or class.")
3. **Dynamically priced offers.** These discounts are offered only for bookings made far in advance or a few hours before an undersold class. Examples:
   - "Last Minute Offers" in the Mindbody App and mindbody.io, where the price of undersold classes drops in the final hours before
   - Dynamically priced offers within ClassPass, where the studio has designated in advance, based on its experience, which classes are more likely to be intrinsically valuable than others
4. **Aggregator offers.** These allow the customer to choose from only a limited set of off-peak offerings such as those routinely sold by ClassPass or Groupon.

In each of these cases, experience has shown that businesses benefit when the cannibalization of full-price-paying customers is minimal.

Differentiated Experiences

As a wellness professional or entrepreneur, you are in the experience business. Whether your target market clients receive your services face to face or via a virtualized digital platform, the value they place on your experiences will be based on the enjoyment and benefits they perceive. If your experiences are very similar to those delivered by your competitors—such as in the hypothetical Studio North and Studio South examples above—then you are selling what economists call a "commodity." Like gasoline, window cleaner, or generic ibuprofen, people will purchase things they perceive to be commodities from the business that is most convenient or lowest priced. Such businesses inevitably have low profits and are not great to be in.

Fortunately, wellness is rarely commoditized. Wellness is a complex concept involving a diverse set of disciplines delivering a wide range of benefits that appeal to a broad range of personal tastes. The fact is, no two wellness classes or appointments are ever precisely the same. As such, there is no reason for anyone to run a commoditized wellness business. Instead, you should differentiate the experience you deliver by appealing to the preferences, needs, and values of your target market client, and you do that by focusing on how you make your clients feel.

> "I've learned that people will forget what you said, people will forget what you did, but people will never forget how you made them feel."
> —— **Maya Angelou**

To understand how feelings relate to differentiated experiences, consider one of the best experience delivery models in the world—Starbucks. In the 1980s, Howard Schultz, the iconic CEO of Starbucks, transformed the cup of coffee from what had been a commoditized product delivered cheaply at diners and convenience stores into a highly differentiated experience that hundreds of millions of people now are willing to spend much more money for.

In his first book, *Pour Your Heart into It: How Starbucks Built a Company One Cup at a Time*, Schultz explains how he did it. Understanding how Howard Schultz transformed an industry through differentiated experiences is the key to designing your own differentiated wellness experiences, and if you haven't read or listened to it already, I highly recommend putting Schultz's book on your list.

Here is a brief summary:

First, Schultz had the breakthrough realization when he was visiting Italy that coffeehouses formed an important *third place* throughout that country—a place where people could gather between home and work to relax and socialize. He used his head, heart, and gut to conclude that this same phenomenon that formed the core of Italian society would work in the United States as well. Wellness businesses are also third places, which is what makes the Starbucks example so relevant.

Schultz was working for the founders of Starbucks, a highly differentiated coffee roaster in Seattle. They didn't even sell brewed or espresso coffee in their original store, except to provide tasting samples to people buying beans. Schultz took his third place insight from Italy back to the United States to transform Starbucks from a local Seattle coffee roaster into a nationwide and then global brand delivering highly differentiated, habit-forming coffee experiences. They built their differentiated third place experiences around the coffee products and the Starbucks coffee houses themselves. Every aspect of a Starbucks is intentional, from the furniture and equipment to the layout, color, smells, and lighting. All of it comes together to deliver an extremely compelling experience quickly and efficiently. If you love Starbucks, you feel happier the moment you walk through the door, long before the coffee even reaches your lips.

That is what your differentiated experience needs to create for your clients. They should feel happier the moment they walk through the door.

To make that happen, Schultz centered the entire Starbucks experience delivery model around their exceptional baristas—all carefully selected, trained, and cared for. Starbucks baristas receive benefits that far exceed equivalent service jobs, including healthcare, 401(k)s, and a free tuition college education through an online university.

There is much more to the Starbucks story. Become a student of Starbucks, studying how they built such an iconic brand and transformed an industry, and you will hone your experience delivery skills.

Enjoyment Is about Brain Chemistry

I don't know if Howard Schultz explicitly understood brain science before he transformed Starbucks from a Seattle coffee roaster into a global phenomenon, but everything he and his team have done, including their rare missteps, demonstrate a deep understanding of the principles of human enjoyment, which is all about brain chemistry.

We modern humans are the descendants of thousands of generations of humans who flourished because they naturally tended to do the things that ensured survival and procreation. To put it in the simplest terms, none of us would be here if our ancestors didn't enjoy forming tribes, securing reliable food and water supplies, creating shelters, caring for each other, choosing mates, producing children, and raising them. The happiness and satisfaction our ancestors derived from doing these things are why we exist at all. And they passed their tendencies on to us.

Everything humans and every other animal does is because it makes them feel good. Perhaps it is easiest to see in another species most of us know well. Anybody who has ever had a dog knows that every choice a dog makes revolves around feeling good. Good dogs want to be close to the humans they are bonded with. They love to eat, sleep, cuddle, and play. They will not only keep us company, they will guard our flocks, eat our leftovers, keep us warm at night, and waken instantly when they perceive a threat. Good dogs will warn us of intruders and attack anything or anyone who threatens us. These natural dog behaviors are governed by their brain chemistry, which our ancestors bred into them to create "man's best friend." Dogs were valuable to our ancestors and are beloved by us today because the actions that make them happy are useful to us and make us happy.

The same is true for human beings. Every day, humans consciously and subconsciously make choices in pursuit of happiness. Understanding how our minds and bodies signal happiness is the key to designing experiences that will draw people to your wellness business.

The Four "Feel Good" Brain Chemicals

Our happy feelings are governed by four chemicals naturally produced inside each of us: dopamine, endorphins, serotonin, and oxytocin. Brain scientists call these "feel good" brain chemicals *neurotransmitters*, and to design a wellness business that attracts and retains long-term clients, you need to learn how to trigger them in your target market clients.

- **Dopamine** is our *reward chemical*. It gives us the joyful rush we feel when we cross a finish line or summit a mountain. It provides the joyful high of falling in love and the excited delight of smelling or tasting something delicious.
- **Endorphins** are our *natural pain killers*. They give us that buzzy natural high we feel after a hard workout and temporarily block the pain of a serious injury. Endorphins enable us to endure extreme exertion when needed and escape from danger when we are injured.
- **Serotonin** is our *confidence chemical*. It is triggered when we are with people we trust and aren't threatened by them. It creates the zone we get into when we are producing our best work. Serotonin causes us to seek safety in numbers.

- **Oxytocin** is our *social bonding chemical*. It provides the openness we feel when we are with someone we trust. Oxytocin causes us to bond socially with others and form committed long-term relationships.

These four neurotransmitters operate in concert to govern nearly every behavior we exhibit and choice we make. It doesn't take a brain scientist to see how these feel good chemicals enabled human beings to flourish. We can picture prehistoric individuals making choices that triggered these feel good chemicals as they successfully fed themselves; fended off predators; created tribes, towns, and cities; and ultimately populated the earth. It is no surprise that in the remaining traditional cultures that exist in our world today, researchers have observed higher levels of happiness than they do in modern society. Our brains are wired to be happier living the way they do.

But for the rest of us living in the modern world, our daily existence has transformed profoundly in a few generations, and our neurotransmitters have not had time to adapt. Today, all manner of feel good triggers involve unhealthy choices, and in many cases those triggers are intentionally designed. Everything from junk foods to flavored tobacco products, to gambling casinos, to violent action movies, to pornography, to social media—all are intentionally designed to trigger our neurotransmitters in a habit-forming way.

If these neurotransmitters sound like drugs, that is no accident. Every mind-altering drug available to us, both legal and illegal, is powerful because it mimics or stimulates the production of our natural feel good neurotransmitters.

Helping People Become Addicted to Wellness

We all know the impact of unhealthy neurotransmitter triggers: obesity, heart disease, type 2 diabetes, and social isolation. This section is about leveraging that insight to steer people toward healthier, happier lives. We are talking about creating habit-forming wellness experiences that addict people to wellness.

This isn't easy because few wellness experiences create instant gratification. Authentic wellness practices require commitment, time, and effort, and many of them are truly difficult to start. For people who are unfit, their first high-intensity workout will make them feel sick and miserable. They may even get physically ill. Endorphins may block some of the pain felt during their first hard workout, but two days later they will feel so sore that it will hurt to move.

Even if they are attending an entry-level class specifically designed with accommodations for beginners, they may still feel embarrassed and can be triggered by a number of situations: putting on tight-fitting exercise clothing, becoming confused on where to go to check in when they enter your business, or feeling awkward as you ask them to move their bodies in ways that are unfamiliar.

How about meditation? For people who have never tried it before, the guidance, mantras, and breathing exercises may be downright annoying, as their conscious minds refuse to let go. Meanwhile, these newbies will notice your other students deeply engaged in something they can't make sense of. They could easily decide meditation is not for them after only one sitting.

With integrative health services, such as therapeutic massages, skin treatments, and acupuncture, the first-time client at least gets to relax while you are treating them. But there are myriad ways the experience may still make them uncomfortable. You may be inviting them to take most or all of their clothes off, let a stranger touch them, or experience moments of discomfort and pain. Let's face it: most wellness experiences are downright intimidating the first time.

For those of us who love taking these classes and receiving these treatments, we feel that love only because our subconscious has connected the experiences to how much better we will feel hours, days, or even weeks later. This prior experience triggers our feel good neurotransmitters when we even think about doing it again, driving our gut to tell our heart that we want to do it again. But the newcomer has no such subconscious memory. To design a wellness business that lasts, it is paramount that you design your experiences from end to end with that in mind.

This is why the wellness industry is still largely serving only a small minority of people. Even today, more than three out of four people are not yet engaging with wellness businesses. With the increasing accessibility of wellness experiences, a large portion of this unengaged majority are likely to embrace wellness practices in the decade ahead. This is where the largest growth opportunities lie and where the next wave of the wellness revolution will come from.

Regardless of whether your target market clients are currently engaged or unengaged with wellness experiences, the way that you will attract them to your business will be by differentiating your experiences with deliberately designed feel good moments. These moments will form the proverbial "bread crumbs" that sustain your target clients through the wellness experiences that will ultimately transform their lives. In a sense, you will fool their neurotransmitters into enjoying something new and challenging long enough for the much deeper rewards of true wellness to begin to kick in.

You will do this by carefully considering how every moment of your experience makes people feel—from the first time they book your experiences online, access your content online, walk through your front door, and interact with your staff. By being that thoughtful in the crafting of your wellness experiences, you will get to know your target market clients even better. You will begin to focus on how you make them feel and that will position you and your business to change their habits and change their lives. Perhaps forever.

This is not easy to do, but when you get it even close to right, you will create rabidly loyal clients who feel so good about your wellness experience that they are booking the next one immediately and spontaneously inviting friends and family as well. That loyalty and spontaneous referral create a powerful flywheel of growth in your business. That is how you create a wellness business that lasts.

You can feel good about hooking your clients on your wellness experiences, because in the process you are giving them more life and you are pulling them up Maslow's hierarchy of needs.

Using the Five Senses to Design "Feel Good" Experiences

As you were reading the words above, you probably already started thinking about how to trigger habit-forming neurotransmitters in your wellness business. You will write those down in a moment, but before you do, think about the impact of our five senses:

- **Smell.** Have you ever smelled something distinctive and had a flood of memories come back? I can't walk onto a Navy ship without being transported decades back in time by the smell alone. It's not unpleasant. The unique combination of oil, hydraulic fluid, electrical wiring, people, and salt water is simply unlike anything I have experienced in normal daily life. When you think about our evolution as human beings, the powerful role of smell makes sense. Scents can travel across distances, reaching us before we come into physical contact with someone or something that is good, bad, enticing, dangerous, or repellant. Scents can also linger in an area, giving us clues as to what happened there before we arrived.
  - In high-end retail stores, hotels, casinos, and first-class airline lounges, pleasant scents are deliberately pumped into the space to shift people's mood, cause them to linger longer, spend money, and yearn to come back. The best wellness businesses are doing this as well.
  - When you think about the scents you want in your space, be mindful of your own scent and that of the people you employ. Give your team members explicit instructions when you hire them. Nothing will ruin a wellness experience faster than an employee who is either wearing too much perfume or cologne or has body odor.
- **Sight.** Our eyes tell us what is happening around us and subconsciously clue us into the nature of the space. A well-ordered, intentionally designed space puts us at ease and focuses our attention where you want it to be—on the wellness experience we just had or are about to have. Conversely, a haphazardly laid out or cluttered space can leave us feeling confused and vaguely ill at ease.
  - Color is an important component of sight, and there is easy-to-find research online on which colors and color combinations will create the mood you want.
  - Light is the medium that transmits the color and other details of a space to our eyes. Whether that light is bright or dim, glaring or diffuse, warm or harsh will dramatically affect how people feel in the space. Simple and inexpensive lighting changes can make an enormous difference in someone's experience.
  - Visit multiple other wellness businesses, as well as other commercial spaces where people gather, such as hotels, restaurants, and high-end retail stores, to note what works and what doesn't. Take careful note of how lighting sets the mood and facilitates the desired interactions.

- Hire an architect and lighting specialist with proven retail experience to lay out your space and plan your lighting design. In addition to the usual discussions with these professionals around uses of space, numbers of people, and traffic flow in and around the space, be sure to explicitly describe the mood you want to set and the feelings you want your clients to have.

- If you are on a very tight budget or are acquiring an existing business you feel is already well laid out, focus on a few color or lighting changes that can further enhance the experience. Replace fluorescent bulbs with the latest-generation LED, which can be dimmed and have the warmer tones people prefer. Install dimmers on every switch, so you can adjust your lighting for different seasons and times of day. Proper lighting doesn't have to be expensive—just well thought out.

- **Touch.** Our skin is our largest organ, and human touch can either be one of our best experiences or our worst. Of course, a wellness practitioner will need to touch us, but so too can a teacher, trainer, or coach. Where and how someone touches us makes all the difference in how that touch is perceived by the recipient.

  - Speaking of touch, there is no excuse for fitness or wellness equipment that is not spotlessly clean. Some people are more tolerant of dirt than others, but nobody is specifically attracted to it. In my twenty years in and around this industry, I have had countless experiences in studios, gyms, and spas that had been allowed to become grimy. Floors should be mopped, linens should be clean, surfaces should be dusted, and the space should be devoid of cobwebs. When one walks into a soiled environment, the only conclusion one can make is poor management. Keeping your wellness business spaces clean is the easiest and least expensive thing to get right. When you or your staff isn't helping a client or working on something else really important, they should be cleaning.

- **Sound.** Having pleasing music or background sounds such as running water or subtle chimes can produce a powerful and memorable experience effect for people. If there are unpleasant sounds intruding through the walls or from the road outside, a white noise generator can mask them without anyone being aware of it. There are multiple apps, like SimplyNoise, that you can download onto your phone to experiment with.

Keeping these sensory points in mind, it's time to describe the experiences you want to create.

Thinking Through Your Differentiated Experiences

Review your target market client description in Chapter 10, and write it down here again:

My target market clients are:

_____

_____

Their unmet needs are:

_____

_____

_____

Now describe how your experiences can release "feel good" neurotransmitters for your clients (write "N/A" if these are not applicable to your wellness practice):

Dopamine. I will trigger dopamine releases in my clients through these rewards (examples: words of affirmation, high fives after class, friendly competitions, public milestone recognition, belts/badges, hot/cold towels, smoothies or power shakes after class):

_____

_____

_____

Endorphins. I will trigger endorphin releases in my clients in these ways (examples: intense exercise sequences, hot saunas and/or cold plunges, non-harmful positions involving moderate pain):

_____

_____

_____

Serotonin. I will trigger serotonin release in my clients in these ways (examples: soothing lighting/décor/music, pleasing scents in the studio, teachers greeting people by name, words of encouragement, after-class socializing):

_____

_____

_____

Oxytocin. I will trigger oxytocin release in my clients in these ways (examples: multiweek wellness challenges, accountability buddies, after-class support groups):

_____

_____

_____

_____

(If you plan to hire others) When I build my team, I will look for these qualities in people who instinctively enjoy delivering the experiences listed above:

_____

_____

_____

_____

These questions should have stirred your creative energies. As you craft your differentiated experiences, know that nothing is cast in stone and perfection is impossible. You can and should commit yourself to regularly collecting client feedback with online survey tools like www.surveymonkey.com and regular client conversations. Apply the insights you gain to regularly evolve your experiences. This is an excellent topic to engage your team with in weekly or monthly staff meetings.

The exciting news for anyone entering the wellness industry is that few wellness businesses operating today are truly nailing it with differentiated experience delivery. The best wellness businesses are optimized for only a portion of their clientele and the worst aren't optimized for anybody. It is not my point to criticize existing wellness business owners. What you do day in and day out is hard. My point is that there are still huge opportunities for innovators to carefully target segments of the market and deliver experiences that delight those audiences.

PART IV

Plan Your Business

13

Create a Vibrant Company Culture with Purpose and Core Values

A company's culture is like the Force in *Star Wars*. It is an unseen but powerful energy that flows in and through everyone who works in the business and to the clients it serves. A company's culture encompasses the purpose, intentions, beliefs, and agreements of the team, clients, and owners. Ultimately, a company's culture is the single greatest determinant of the value it delivers to its clients and the value it creates for its owners.

Companies with a truly vibrant culture infused with purpose, leadership, and values have a huge advantage over their competitors. Their chances of long-term success are much better than for businesses with only average cultures. Furthermore, in this day when talent is in far shorter supply than jobs, any company lacking a high-functioning culture is doomed to fail, regardless of its current size, funding, and product set. Culture is that important.

For the independent practitioner, you are your company. Your personality, expertise, charisma, and commitment to craft define your company culture. Even being an independent practitioner is your ultimate objective, I strongly recommend reading this chapter and completing its exercises. These exercises will cause you to record the feelings, motivations, and beliefs that are driving the formation of your wellness business, giving you a crucial North Star in the Hero's Journey ahead. If you do plan to hire people, you will need to build a vibrant culture that attracts the right people to your team and inspires them to produce their best work. Creating that culture is done by defining your business with a purpose greater than itself and an explicitly stated set of actionable core values that you and your team will practice every day.

Defining Your Purpose

Businesses that last are not created just to make money. Being profitable is important, but if that is your only purpose, the business will soon feel empty, even to you and any other owners making money from the business.

As human beings we crave purpose in our lives, and businesses that last must give us that or our hearts will soon move on. Your purpose needs to be authentically crafted by you and your co-founders, if you have them, and it must be clearly and succinctly stated. Great businesses call these short but powerful manifestos *purpose statements, vision statements, mission statements*, or perhaps simply *Our Why*. Personally, I prefer *purpose statement* because it plainly states what it is.

Regardless of what you call your statement, it must tell your team, your clients, and any potential investors why your business deserves to exist in the world. Here are some excellent examples of effective purpose statements:

> *To organize all the world's information and make it universally accessible and useful*—Google
>
> *To build a place where people come to find anything they might want to buy online*—Amazon
>
> *To help people lead healthier, happier lives by connecting the world to wellness*—Mindbody
>
> *To accelerate the advent of sustainable energy*—Tesla
>
> *To save our home planet*—Patagonia

Notice what these purpose statements have in common:

- They address a fundamental need of large numbers of people and in doing so make the world a better place. That is what draws us to these businesses and their products.

- They are distinctive. While there are businesses that compete with each of these companies, they do not approach market opportunities in quite the same way.
- They are authentic. Go to each of these company's websites, look at what they do, and you will quickly see that they are actually acting on their purpose.
- They are succinct. When powerful ideas are stated with the least amount of words, people remember them.
- They are timeless. Purpose statements are not destinations. They are the star that these businesses steer their ship by. None of these purpose statements will be completed in their founders' lifetimes. But these powerful words will attract wave after wave of purpose-driven people inspired to achieve them.

Preparing to Write Your Purpose Statement

Are you ready to craft your inspiring purpose statement? As a fellow wellness entrepreneur, I have great news. You're already halfway there. Wellness itself is inspiring!

Whether you are aspiring simply to be self-employed as an independent or virtual wellness professional, or a full-fledged entrepreneur employing others, it is paramount that you craft your purpose statement. Once crafted, this statement will make every other decision you make easier.

Take a few minutes and jot down the first thoughts that come into your mind when you read these questions. If you are considering a partnership, then every one of your prospective partners should do this exercise independently. (You can complete this exercise in the book or on a notepad. Either way, I highly recommend old school pen and paper.)

1. What is motivating me to focus my career around the wellness industry?
   _____
   _____
   _____

2. What kinds of people do I want to serve?
   _____
   _____
   _____

3. What do I understand about these people that isn't obvious?

_____

_____

_____

4. I'll know I'm fulfilling my purpose when . . .

_____

_____

_____

_____

_____

Read through your responses to these questions and circle those that are most meaningful. We will call these "key words and phrases." Now we'll expand on those.

Copy your circled words or phrases into the "key word/phrase" lines below or onto a new set of sticky notes. In the space below each word or phrase, write down additional concepts each brings to mind. (*Hint*: Search your words online and look for synonyms, antonyms, and definitions to stimulate your thinking.)

Key word/phrase: _____

_____

Key word/phrase: _____

_____

Key word/phrase: _____

_____

Key word/phrase: _____

_____

Key word/phrase: _____

_____

Key word/phrase: _____

_____

Key word/phrase: _____

_____

Key word/phrase: _____

_____

Now using the Voice Memos app on your phone, or a similar recording device, read these words out loud, and start talking about what they mean to you. Why do you care about these words? What images do they bring to mind?

Crafting Your Purpose Statement

Before you craft your purpose statement, consider these guidelines:

- An effective purpose statement should have no defined timeline. It should still inspire and motivate people ten years from now.
- Your purpose statement should explain the benefits your company will deliver to your community or the world and may broadly describe how you will deliver these benefits. But it should not prescribe specific methods. For example, the closing words of Mindbody's purpose statement ("by connecting the world to wellness") explains how we are helping people lead healthier, happier lives, but they do not prescribe how those connections will be made because consumer habits and technologies are constantly evolving. The same will likely be true in your business.
- Use strong verbs to add power to your purpose—words like *organize, elevate, build, save, improve, help, revolutionize,* and *lead.*
- In your first draft, don't worry about length. Write down everything that comes to mind in the space below or in a notebook.

The purpose of my business is to . . .

_____

_____

_____

_____

_____

_____

_____

_____

_____

Once you have written down your thoughts, but not earlier, you may loop in a trusted friend or acquaintance to help you craft your first-draft purpose statement. A business's purpose must reflect the authentic intentions of its founders and co-founders.

After you are satisfied that you have captured the bulk of what is in your head, heart, and gut, start consolidating unnecessary and redundant ideas to end up with a purpose statement of not more than 20 words; 8-12 words is ideal.

Write your first-draft purpose statement (not to exceed 20 words) here:

_____

_____

_____

_____

_____

Congratulations! Now you have a concise and meaningful purpose statement. You may decide to refine it later if you feel compelled to, and if grammar and spelling are not your strong suit, then have a friend proofread it. Most likely the 15–20 words you just wrote down are enough to guide you on the road ahead.

Now type that purpose statement in a large font on a large piece of paper and post it somewhere where you will see it every day. When you launch your website, be sure to feature your purpose statement prominently. And when you start hiring people, be sure to talk about your purpose statement and ask them how it can be meaningful in their lives.

Defining Your Actionable Core Values

Core values feel like an abstract concept to many people and this is precisely why they must be explicitly defined. The values of an organization are in fact the defining difference between those organizations that last and those that don't. These values won't require everyone to think alike. To the contrary, a diversity of perspectives combined with an atmosphere that encourages team members to share their points of view in a constructive way are the hallmarks of long-term success.

In a business, constructive collaboration is not possible if every decision turns into a laborious congressional or parliamentary debate. To have both collaboration and agility, a business must have a team that can quickly reach consensus on most things because they are aligned on their most important principles and values. Those principles and values must be defined and embodied by the founders of the business. Core values definition is not a moment for democracy. As with your purpose statement, if the founders don't know what you stand for, how can I as your future employee know?

Four Qualities of Actionable Core Values

These four qualities will make your core values meaningful and impactful to your business:

1. **They connect to your purpose.** To be coherent, your core values need to extend outward from your purpose, describing the team needed to achieve it. When you state your core values, you lay the groundwork of how your purpose will be achieved.
2. **They are authentic.** Your core values will be prominently displayed on your website and in your place of business. To be meaningful, those values must accurately reflect the founder or founders. While it's not realistic for anyone to be their best selves 100% of the time, a core values statement that clearly diverges from the personalities and demonstrated behaviors of the founders will quickly be dismissed as irrelevant by team members and customers alike.
3. **They are distinctive.** Your core values should be both inspiring and challenging to everyone who reads them. Easy bromides like "honest," "punctual," or "customer centric" are impossible to argue against and therefore not distinctive enough to attract the people you want and repel those you don't. Both outcomes are important, as one misaligned team member will drain your energy and damage your business. Two misaligned team members in a small business can destroy it.
4. **They are practiced.** If you aren't willing to hire, develop, and let go of people based on core values, then those values aren't worth anything. You can correct someone's work habits and teach them new skills. But you cannot change who they are. Who they are is embodied in their core values, which were likely set in their childhood.

Crafting Your Core Values

Now that we understand the importance and qualities of actionable core values, let's craft them. As with your purpose statement, if you are considering a partnership, then every one of your prospective partners should do this exercise independently.

Here or in your notebook, write down the first responses that come into your mind:

1. People who will be inspired by our purpose tend to have these characteristics:

   _____

   _____

   _____

2. The most successful people I've known in my life have these characteristics:

   _____

   _____

   _____

   _____

   _____

3. The least successful people I've known in my life have these characteristics:

   _____

   _____

   _____

4. I love working with people who . . .

   _____

   _____

   _____

5. I can't stand working with people who . . .

   _____

   _____

   _____

Circle the key words and phrases that pop out, both positive and negative. Either alone or together with your prospective business partners, make two columns on a white board or piece of easel paper with these headings:

Qualities We Want in Our Team	Qualities We Don't Want in Our Team

For the qualities you don't want, use an online thesaurus to define the antonyms or opposites of those qualities. For example, if you wrote down *arrogant,* the top two antonyms are *humble* and *modest.* Pick the one or two you like best. Now add those antonyms in the left-hand column.

Now combine like words and phrases and cross out those that are redundant. This should leave you with a list of 10–20 words or phrases.

If you have multiple partners, give each partner an opportunity to veto one core value. If those vetoes cause heartache for another partner and involve more than 8 qualities on your list, use a voting system to identify those that are most important to you. You can do this with sticky dots or sharpies. Each co-founder gets 10 votes, and they can distribute those votes however they choose.

At Mindbody, we didn't craft our first core values statement until we had been operating for more than six years. This was during a time when Blake wasn't working in the business, so I wrote them and asked a group of about a dozen people out of our team of 150, people who had been with the business for multiple years and who I considered to be the core of our company culture, to comment. Producing that first core values statement benefited us in multiple ways.

Ten years later, we pulled together a cross-functional team of 60 people out of our global team of more than 1,500, people who were nominated by their peers who best embodied Mindbody's purpose and values, and asked them to update and refine our core values statement. I think the revisions that came out of that process were excellent, and they kept closely to our original principles with important refinements that reflected what we had learned about organizational effectiveness through the years.

At Mindbody, our core values have been an essential element of our success since our days in the garage. Their precise wording and emphasis have evolved through the years, but the underlying principles closely reflect beliefs Blake and I held dear more than twenty years ago. Mindbody's core values are shown below as an example for you to work with. Feel free to lift any portion of them that resonate with you.

Mindbody's Core Values

Committed to Wellness

Embracing the Seven Dimensions of Wellness
   Driven by a purpose greater than ourselves and dedicated to the wellness industry

Caring for ourselves, others, and our planet so future generations may thrive in this amazing place

Leading lives that harmonize responsibilities, relationships, recreation, and rest

Remembering to have fun and taking actions to create and sustain happiness

Audaciously Achieving

Inspired by MINDBODY's bold purpose

Passionate about strong, sustainable growth for our clients and our business

Driven to achieve through commitment, focus, creativity, and grit

Displaying integrity in word and action

Holding ourselves and our teams accountable for results

Humble & Helpful

Recognizing and cherishing the humanity in all people

Caring as much for others as we do for ourselves

Hearing and respecting everyone's ideas, so we may all contribute and learn

Empathetic

Striving to understand the perspective of others

Sharing the journey of our clients, our consumers, and our company

Helping the people we serve achieve their dreams with power and confidence

Consciously Evolving

Recognizing that each of us is completely free to wake up and be just a little bit better

Taking actions to evolve MINDBODY so we remain valuable in our vigorously competitive landscape

Keeping our minds open, knowing that inspiration may come from anywhere

A Vibrant Culture Is Never Static

As entrepreneurs, we define the culture we want our companies to have and we take actions to shape our business in that direction. But the cultures we create will not remain static. A company is an organism, and it must evolve and grow to thrive. You will know it is working when your team embraces your culture and begins to take your business beyond where even you imagined it could go.

At Mindbody, the manifestations of this are too numerous to count – employee-led initiatives that have reinforced our purpose and elevated our company culture. None of these are more inspiring than our grassroots Equality, Diversity, and Inclusivity affinity groups. Several years ago, a group of women engineers created a Mindbody Women in Technology group. They did this spontaneously with no prompting from me or our other leaders. That group of volunteers began working in our local schools to inspire girls to learn computer science, and before long they were actively recruiting other women engineers to join Mindbody. Their efforts have not only made Mindbody a better place for all women to work, but they have attracted hundreds more women in technology to our team.

A few years later, a group of Mindbody team members created Mindbody Pride to empower and support LGBTQ+ team members. Their volunteer efforts have made Mindbody a more welcoming place, attracted top talent to us, and inspired all of us to become better people.

A few years after that, a group of Mindbody veterans created Mindbody Vets, an affinity group that highlights and honors the capabilities and experiences of our team members who served in the armed forces. Mindbody Vets has donated time and supplies to aid homeless veterans, sponsored bootcamp-style workouts, and attracted countless more highly talented veterans to our team.

And in 2019 a group of our team members created Mindbody United with the goal of increasing diversity across our team, particularly for people of color. Less than a year later, when the killings of Ahmaud Arbery, George Floyd, and others sparked global protests against racism and the mistreatment of Black people, it was our Mindbody United affinity group that inspired and guided our leadership team as we raised our voices in support of Black Lives Matter.

Such a culture is truly vibrant and alive. It has transcended the founder and is capable of living on far beyond the founder's tenure. This is a culture of a wellness business that lasts. There is nothing more gratifying as an entrepreneur than to see this happen.

14

Design Your Role

As an entrepreneur you have the unique opportunity to design your business and your role in that business at the same time. As a founder or co-founder, you don't have to be the boss. Some of the most successful entrepreneurs realized early on that they did not enjoy the demands of being president or CEO. If your objective is to build something that can run without you within a few years, you will need to place someone else in charge early on.

To make these key decisions, you will need to first understand your own motivation and time horizon. If you are going into business with one or more partners, each of you will need to come to this understanding together.

Defining Your Motivations and Time Horizon

The entrepreneurial journey is a challenging one. How ambitious are you and how long do you want to be engaged with the business you are creating?

These questions get at the root of your true motivation in forming your business, the personal price you are willing to pay to achieve success, and the amount of time you willing to give it. These are your motivations and your time horizon.

Your motivation measures how much energy you are willing to devote on a daily basis to your wellness business. At the high end of the motivation spectrum are those ambitious people motivated by achievement. They are willing to invest a great deal of time to create successful businesses and are willing to sacrifice a portion of their personal time and freedom to achieve that success. At the other end of the motivation spectrum are those who place a high priority on their personal time and freedom. They want to create a successful wellness business, but they do not want to sacrifice much of their personal time for family, friends, travel, and hobbies to do it.

Your time horizon expresses the length of time in years that you are willing to devote to the wellness business you are planning to build. At the high end of this spectrum are those looking to create their life's work: long-term businesses they hope to focus on for most or all of their professional careers. At the other end of the spectrum are those looking for a near-term source of income or value creation.

If we visualize *Motivation* and *Time Horizon* in a matrix, we see the results shown in Figure 14.1. In the upper-right-hand quadrant we find long-term

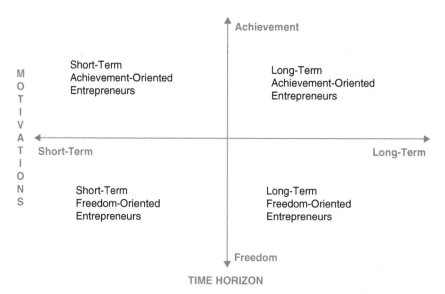

Figure 14.1   Motivation and Time Horizon Matrix

achievement-oriented entrepreneurs. I know these people well because I am one of them.

Long-Term Achievement-Oriented Entrepreneurs

Since childhood my motivations have always skewed strongly toward long-term goals and high achievement. For reasons I cannot fully explain, I am driven to achieve—going to the Naval Academy, becoming a nuclear submarine officer, and growing Mindbody from the garage to a global company. There is some fire burning deep inside to tackle hard things that take a long time to reach fruition.

Given this ambition, when we launched Mindbody I had very high expectations of myself, the business, and Blake. People often ask me today, "Did you believe in your garage that Mindbody would be so successful?" Yes! After learning about the rapidly emerging wellness market, the generally weak competition, and Blake's compelling product, I was confident that Mindbody would be a valuable global business one day. Had I not believed that I would never have risked my time and money to take the leap.

My motivation and time horizon sustained me for twenty years, before I decided to hand the baton off and transition to the less demanding role of Executive Chairman. Nevertheless, my ambition hasn't changed. I am still seeking out new challenges. One of these is the writing of this book.

My mom passed away last year after a multi-year battle with cancer. It was a gut-wrenching time for our family, but I am most thankful that I was able to spend meaningful time with her right up until she passed. One of the last things she and I talked about was my intention to write this book. I told her about all of you—the wellness professionals and entrepreneurs I had come to know so well—and how I hoped to produce something for you that really mattered, something that could help you avoid the common pitfalls and realize your dreams.

I must have gotten pretty animated, because my mom looked at me with a knowing smile and said, "I don't know where you get all that energy."

Neither do I, Mom. But I do know that this is exactly the journey my soul wants to be on. That is what makes me a long-term achievement-oriented entrepreneur.

But that may not be you.

Short-Term Achievement-Oriented Entrepreneurs

Short-term achievement-oriented entrepreneurs are people who tend to have high creative capacity. They have a unique ability to intensely focus on hard problems and they often come up with breakthrough ideas that excite them. But they rarely have the desire to run the resulting businesses that those ideas fuel for more than a few years. Artists, inventors, and serial entrepreneurs are often found in this group. One of those I know very well is my Mindbody co-founder, Blake Beltram.

Mindbody sprang from Blake's original idea. Blake saw the boutique yoga, Pilates, and Spinning® movement emerging in Los Angeles in the late 1990s; realized these businesses had unique operational challenges that databases, software, and the Internet could resolve; and taught himself how to code. He created the first software application, named it HardBody Software, and installed it in multiple studios before I even got involved.

In early 2001, just a few months after we launched HardBody Software, LLC, Blake and I spent several days together visiting our early adopter customers in southern California. This was a golden time for me. Everything in the business was new and I had fallen in love with our customers. I loved their grass-roots entrepreneurial spirit, their fierce independence, and their gritty determination to succeed. They reminded me of my family. I loved the transformational impact of the classes they taught and the wellness services they provided. In those early months, I began to fully understand the vast opportunity in front of us. We were early movers in a potentially huge small business market with few competitors and myriad ways to create value. Most of the things you see Mindbody doing today were conceived by Blake and me in those early months.

At the same time the tough challenges of our startup were coming into sharp focus. The hard truth was that most of our early customers weren't happy. Our software had lots of bugs and there were huge technical challenges to surmount before we would be able to fully deliver the functionality they wanted. It would take years of focused effort to meet their expectations and we realized, in fact, that the software would never be done.

On the last night of our trip, sitting in a bar in downtown Glendale, Blake said to me, "You know . . . this isn't my life's work. There are other things I want to go do." I looked at my dear friend, this guy I had known since high school, and saw his truth. Blake was an original thinker. Conceiving and launching HardBody Software had energized him, both the zoomed-in granular detail of creating the product and the zoomed-out conception of a grand business vision.

After two years of dealing with demanding customers and difficult-to-eradicate bugs, he had grown exhausted with the business. He had fallen out of love with it. I didn't realize it at the time, but the thought of multiple more years of hard labor to realize our grand vision felt soul crushing to Blake. But I didn't feel that way at all. In that instant I realized and stated my simple truth: "Well, this might be my life's work! I am really loving this, despite all the challenges."

Blake and I were both high achievers and big thinkers. We were unified by our common desire to create something that really mattered, but we were on completely different pages with our time horizons. Blake wanted to apply his unique insight to create a meaningful business in a few years so that he could sell that business and move on to something else. I wanted to dig into the business for at least a decade. My greatest hope was to build Mindbody into something large enough to exercise the business leadership skills I believe I had. I wasn't likely to be hired to run a large software company. I had to build it, and I was yearning to find my life's work.

In many ways, ours was a match made in heaven. I could not have dreamed up an original business idea as cool and impactful as Mindbody, and Blake had little interest in the multi-year journey to transform that idea into a global brand.

In that conversation, we agreed that Blake would stay in the business for another year or so before moving on. But we didn't talk about how to gradually reduce Blake's role in the business or how I would one day buy him out so that he could exit with the money he needed to pursue his next venture.

The mistake we made that week was not writing down our new understanding and not engaging a business attorney to amend our partnership agreement accordingly. Our failure to do that ultimately led to two unhappy years of strained partnership, followed by several months of legal conflict and a painful breakup. Our acrimonious breakup severely damaged our friendship for years and nearly destroyed a great business. Remember my metaphor about lawyers and dentists (Chapter 9)? We didn't get our preventive care.

Thankfully, Blake and I did ultimately reconcile. We rebuilt our friendship, and I invited Blake to return to the business for several years in a role that matched his creative entrepreneurial nature. Blake became the *Mindbody Evangelist*, engaging directly with our customers to improve our products and acting as a sparkplug to ignite multiple impactful projects, such as www.mindbody.one, our customer user group community.

But all of that could have happened much more gracefully had we understood our differing time horizons up front.

Freedom-Oriented Entrepreneurs

Blake's and my personalities may not resonate with you at all. You may dream of a wellness business that supports your lifestyle and doesn't require you to sacrifice your personal priorities. You may want to home school your kids or coach their sports teams. Or you may want to spend more time with elderly parents or a significant other. Or you may simply want more time to pursue your hobbies, explore the world, or deepen your spiritual path. Either way, it's personal freedom you are looking for, and you will want your wellness business to support that. You want a lifestyle business.

Such lifestyle businesses include most independent wellness professionals, who vary their work schedules to fit their personal needs. These include the itinerant professionals, such as the yoga teachers, fitness instructors, and massage therapists who can practice their craft virtually anywhere. Many of them live an idyllic life of traveling the world and working intermittently to support their simple lives.

This is a key point. If the life of freedom-oriented wellness entrepreneur appeals to you, keep your personal life as simple as possible and embrace the immutable truth that nothing worthwhile is achieved without effort. There are no free lunches or easy riches. To believe otherwise is to set yourself up for unhappiness and frustrated goals.

Pick your passion: sports, politics, mountain climbing, marriage, parenthood, or spiritual growth. If it's worthwhile, it will be challenging, because the challenge is what makes the pursuit so satisfying. If ease were the measure of an activity's desirability, then the game of golf would have been designed with the ball starting six inches from the cup. Who would play that game?

I'm taking the time to make this point because I have met a few wellness professionals through the years who get tripped up on this. They believe that a life well lived should be effortless. They believe that struggle is an indicator that someone is on the wrong path. Such people have never built successful businesses.

When you are launching a business, you are not sitting on a mountaintop gazing at the scenery. You are building a road to the mountaintop. To believe otherwise is to set yourself up for a life of frustrated goals and disappointment.

One poignant example are those who get pulled into multi-level marketing schemes. We've all heard the pitch: buy into someone else's pyramid and then recruit your friends, family, and neighbors to buy into yours. Soon you will have built a passive income stream that pays you every time somebody in your down chain purchases a vacation or household product. Soon you will never have to work again. If that sounds too good to be true that's because it is.

The truth is multi-level marketing schemes cannot create passive income for anyone, other than the very few at the top of the pyramid, and even those people will find themselves working desperately hard to keep their pyramid from crumbling. This is because multi-level marketing violates a fundamental economic principle: in a free market every step in the value delivery chain must continuously add value or it will be disintermediated. Said another way, in a free market, middlemen adding no value are soon squeezed out. The levels in a multi-level marketing chain create cost, not value.

If a lifestyle business is what you want, then follow the principles of this book. Conceive of an innovative, highly profitable business model that you can work at intermittently, or hire others to operate it. If you want a truly passive income, one where you check in on your business only occasionally, then be ready to invest years of effort and many dollars to get that business to a place where it can pay you even when you aren't working.

The Four Common Entrepreneurial Types

Figure 14.2 shows how the four most common entrepreneurial personas are positioned in the *Motivation and Time Horizon matrix*.

> **Brand Creators.** These are the founders and CEOs of global or regional wellness brands. Many of these brands have played a pivotal role in the development of the wellness industry, accelerated consumer adoption, and become household names.
>
> **Neighborhood Business Owners.** The proprietors of successful local wellness businesses still make up the majority of the industry today. They are either independently conceived by their founders, or they are franchisees of larger brands. Either way, the owners may be full-time operators, or they may hire others to manage their businesses, providing them with a passive income.
>
> **Independent Professionals.** These are wellness practitioners who either flex their hours weekly to balance their personal needs or work intermittently to earn the income they need to support their freedom-oriented life.

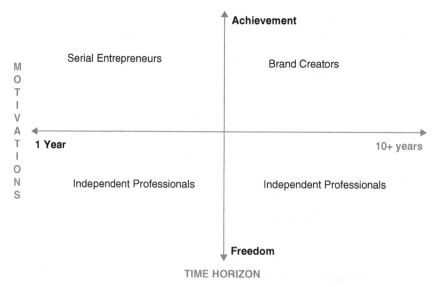

Figure 14.2   Four Entrepreneurial Types

Serial Entrepreneurs. These are another rare breed who have the knack for quickly identifying, formulating, and launching successful businesses. They get those engines started, then sell them to others and go off to start another.

These four personas typify most of the wellness industry today. Your plans may be different, and in fact a virtual wellness business could exist in any of the four quadrants. The point of this is for you to reflect and estimate where you fall today. If you have a business partner, it is essential that you both answer these questions:

1. What does business success mean to you?
   _____
   _____
   _____

2. On a scale of 1 to 10, with 1 being "Not at all" and 10 being "I'll do whatever it takes to succeed," how much are you willing to sacrifice your personal priorities right now to realize your definition of business success? _____

3. How many years are you willing to focus on this business to achieve your definition of success? (1–10 years) _____

If you are divergent in your motivation levels, you may need to reconsider your partnership. Operating partners may have differing work styles or schedules; one may be an early riser and the other a night owl, for example. One may like to grind hard for a few days, then rest, then grind hard again, while the other may be more of a steady worker. If two operating partners differ widely in their desire to achieve and their willingness to work hard, their partnership will soon be strained. This cannot be fixed just by agreeing to different salaries, because the majority of the value you are creating will likely be in the terminal value of your ownership.

15

Select Your Integrated Software and Payments Platform

Regardless of the size of your wellness business, you will need a business management software platform to manage your customer relationships, take their online bookings, and associate those bookings with their purchases. If you plan to employ staff, you will need software to help you schedule, manage, and pay them as well. You will also need a payments platform to accept electronic credit or debit card payment, and it will be far more beneficial is these two business critical systems are integrated with each other.

To be "integrated" means that your business management and payments platforms talk to each other. That means regardless of how and when your client pays you, whether online or at your front desk, a record of that sale is automatically created in your business management software as their payment is authorized for deposit into your bank account. An integrated software and payments platform also enables you to easily set up recurring memberships and schedule automatic monthly payments ("autopays") that continue to process for the lifetime of the membership with little or no additional effort on your part.

Payment processing costs money. Depending on the types of credit or debit cards processed and the method of payment—"card present," where clients insert their card chip into your credit card machine in front of you, or "card not present," where they key in the card digits via a web or mobile interface—you can expect to pay about 2–3% of your sales in merchant processing fees. These fees can add up to quite a lot, but they are well worth the cost. Your only other alternative is to run your business accepting only cash or paper checks.

We have all been customers of small businesses that run on cash payments only, and this idea may seem attractive at first. But the allure of a "cash only business" is a siren on the rocks. It is both attractive and dangerous. In the wellness industry the payment processing fees you avoid will be eclipsed tenfold by the clients and revenue you miss out on. And for those who intend to duck the money, this is a good point for a reminder that under-reporting business revenue to the government is illegal and not worth it. If you get into the habit of doing this, you will always be looking over your shoulder in fear of stiff penalties or criminal prosecution. To build a wellness business that lasts, one that can receive bank or investor financing one day, and one that can be ultimately sold to another entrepreneur, it is far better to conduct your business above board, reporting all of the revenue you receive.

The Mindbody team and I understood all of this when we started our business in my garage more than twenty years ago. And we are not the only ones. Today, there are dozens of integrated software and payments platforms suitable for boutique wellness businesses. Many of these are quite good, but obviously I believe Mindbody's is the best. So rather than comparing Mindbody to its competitors, I will describe the features and capabilities you should expect from your integrated software and payments provider.

Key Software Platform Requirements

The key capabilities that any wellness business software should have are listed below. You should use this list when shopping for your solution.

1. **Client relationship management** that records your clients' contact information, as well as emergency contacts and relationships they

have with other clients (e.g., spouses, significant others, employers, parent/child). This system should also enable you to assign categories and client types to different people so that you can easily identify members of different groups (e.g., people you connected to at the Kiwanis wellness event you spoke at last month) for later reporting and marketing. This system should safely store your clients' encrypted credit card and direct debit payment methods, as well as their history of purchases, classes, and appointments received; current active passes or memberships; and future schedules.

2. **Staff management** that stores your staff biographies and photos, as well as their qualifications and certifications to lead certain classes or deliver certain services, enabling that key information to be automatically published to your web and mobile online booking systems. Your staff management software should also have a timeclock function. Hourly rates should be recorded when staff are on the clock, as well as their variable compensation based on the value of the appointments they deliver, number of people taught in a class, and any bonuses or sales commissions they earn. Variable compensation is important in the wellness industry as it encourages your staff members to contribute to the growth of your wellness business. There are dozens of little things they can do with your clients each day to encourage them to purchase more classes or appointments.

3. **Class scheduling** that stores your class names, descriptions, capacities, categories, and photos. This system should enable you to manage waitlists for popular classes, automatically upgrading and notifying waitlisted people when others cancel. It should allow you to easily replace a regularly scheduled teacher with a substitute and allow you to cancel classes due to weather, holidays, or teacher unavailability. All of this should seamlessly publish to your website and mobile apps and update in real time so that your classes are never overbooked.

4. **Appointment scheduling** where you define and describe the services you and your staff provide, including appointment descriptions, types of services, lengths of services, and the required prep and finish times between appointments. This software should also define who is qualified to deliver which services and how much allotted time each practitioner requires to complete those services. This software should enable easy appointment add-ons (e.g., adding aromatherapy to a massage) and be able to reserve resources—such as rooms, chairs, or tables—for the appointment. Your appointment software should be able to book a professional with more than one client at a time, such as

with a semi-private personal training, or book two practitioners with one client, such as with a two-on-one massage, or book groups such as wedding parties, spa days, or couples massages.

5. **Enrollment tracking** that allows clients to book and pay for special single-day or multi-day events, such as workshops, retreats, or certification programs. Because these events tend to be more expensive than regular classes, your enrollment software should be able to accept client pre-booking with a deposit or payment plan and track client attendance in a multi-session program.

6. **Integrated online booking** that automatically enables you to take client bookings and payments from yours or any partner's web or mobile app interface. It stands to reason that the more places people can find and discover your business and actually engage with you, even if you are off-duty or asleep, the more clients will be drawn to your business and the more successful you will become. For your wellness business to flourish, it should be as easy for people to find your services as it is for them to book their plane ticket to London and the hotel they will be staying at when they get there.

7. **An integrated paywall-protected virtual wellness platform** that enables wellness businesses to seamlessly deliver classes and appointments to their clients face-to-face or remotely via livestreamed classes or on-demand libraries.

8. **Contracts and autopay software** that enables you to sell memberships, auto-reloading class passes, and other auto-renewing packages. This system should enable you to store your contract terms and conditions so those can be reviewed by and agreed to electronically by your clients. The system should store clients' payment information for scheduled auto-pay authorizations. This system should automatically submit the credit card or direct debit transactions to your integrated payments gateway at the predetermined time, manage any rejected authorizations, notify clients when their stored credit cards are about to expire, and enable them to update their payment information without you having to be involved.

9. **Point of sale and inventory management (POS/IM)** that enables you to manage a retail store inside your wellness business, seamlessly collecting client payments for classes and appointments. Your POS/IM should integrate online and face-to-face transactions into one sales and sales tax reporting system and be fully functional for all products and services your business will need to sell, including dynamic and statically priced services, multi-session passes, membership sales and upgrades, paying for another client, and gift cards. Your POS should

store regular selling prices and cost of goods sold and should seamlessly apply discounts, promotion codes, sales taxes, and value-added tax. Finally, your POS should manage your product inventory, automatically triggering purchases when inventory levels reach predetermined reorder points so that you never run out of a popular product.

10. **POS/IM hardware devices** required to complete all of the above, including credit card chip readers, receipt printers, cash drawers, price tag label printers, and bar code scanners for quick retail checkout and rapid taking of physical inventory. This hardware should easily connect to any PC, Mac, smartphone, iPad, or tablet via Bluetooth or USB connection.

11. **Robust dashboards and reports** that enable you to understand what is happening in your business. They enable your bookkeeper and accountant to easily prepare your financial statements and tax returns.

12. **A business-facing mobile app for iPhones and Androids.** Your business apps should work on whichever phone type you have, extending key functionality to you and your staff when you're on the go. At a minimum, your business mobile app should enable you and your designated staff to manage your business, change schedules, book clients, and keep tabs on your business anytime, anywhere. Suppose you are at a dinner party and somebody wants to have a session with you. They reach into their wallet and hand you a credit card. You should be able to pull out your smart phone, book them into their first class or appointment, and record their payment information in under two minutes. Alternatively, suppose you are sitting on a beach in Maui. You should be able to pick up your phone in between sips of your tropical drink and check a mobile dashboard to see how much money your team made you that day.

13. **A consumer-facing branded mobile app** that places your brand on the home screen of hundreds or thousands of your clients' smartphones. Like the Starbucks app now initiates the majority of all coffee purchases at Starbucks around the world, your branded mobile app should keep your clients engaged with your business, prompting them to purchase more wellness.

14. **Full integration with your payments platform** as discussed above.

Key Integrated Payments Platform Requirements

There are dozens of payments processors around the world positioning themselves as suitable for wellness businesses. Your commercial bank may even try to push a payments solution on to you. But most of these providers cannot meet your needs or help you build a wellness business that lasts, unless they can offer the following:

1. **Full integration with your software platform** so that every credit or debit card authorization and settlement is connected to your business management sales records, regardless of whether that sale originates inside your physical place of business, at a remote event, or from your website or mobile app.
2. **Real-time tracking and reporting of all payments authorizations, batch settlements, and deposits** so that you and your bookkeeper can easily reconcile your bank account and follow up on any payments that are held up by the processor.
3. **Card Present and Card Not Present capabilities** so that all client payments, regardless if they are processed face-to-face, online, or from a scheduled auto-pay membership, deposit in the same manner into a single business checking account.
4. **Contactless payment and e-wallet capability** so that your clients can easily spend money on your business.
5. **Clear and easy fee reporting** so that you can anticipate how much cash you will actually receive into your checking account.
6. **Chargeback defense** where the payments processor helps you resolve disputes with your clients and receive the money rightfully due to you.

These integrated software and payments platform features are table stakes for wellness businesses and as you've probably guessed, Mindbody has all of them. Mindbody also has the best phone-based training and support, as well as the largest network of independent consultants to help you successfully launch a wellness business that lasts on our platform.

While you may not need all of these capabilities in the initial conception of your wellness business, your concepts may change and you'll want to pick a software platform that can grow and evolve with you. Swapping out your software and payments platform after your business is launched is hard. It is far better to hitch your wagon to a horse that can support you regardless of how your business evolves.

The Importance of Future-Proofing

When you choose an integrated software and payments platform provider, you aren't just betting on their current capabilities; you are betting on their capacity to continue improving those capabilities for many years to come. The beauty of modern cloud software is that improvements happen much more rapidly than they did in prior decades, and those improvements are generally made available to everyone using the cloud platform. Your software and payments provider needs to have the financial capacity and the organizational will to continue investing in those improvements.

To keep up with business owner and consumer expectations, Mindbody has consistently reinvested more than 20 percent of its revenue into ongoing product development. Even in the face of COVID-19, Mindbody protected and prioritized its product development roadmap, funneling nearly 30 percent of revenue—more than $70 million in 2020 alone—into cutting-edge product improvements. This commitment enabled the Mindbody Team to early release and rapidly improve its groundbreaking Virtual Wellness Platform in the early months of the COVID crisis. Because Mindbody has the largest base of business customers in the world and serves more leading wellness brands than anyone else, you can bet that they will invest more in product development in the 2020s than in any prior decade.

Regardless of who you choose as your software platform partner, be sure to ask them how much they spent on product development in the prior year and how much they are budgeting in the years ahead. Any software platform that remains static in the 2020s will be hopelessly out of date before long.

Software Buying Mistakes

Software Buying Mistake #1: Choosing Your Platform Based on Price Alone

Living deep in the twenty-first century, we have become accustomed to incredibly powerful cloud software and other technologies that are extremely inexpensive or even free to use. These include nearly every search engine, mapping tool, weather app, and social media site in use today. Have you ever wondered why Google, Facebook, Twitter, Instagram, YouTube, TikTok, and Pinterest are free? The answer is found in the most important truth of the information age:

If you aren't paying for the product, you are the product.

What these tech giants and many others have in common is a business model built around enticing us to use their powerful products and then selling our behavior and attention to others. There's nothing inherently wrong with this. It's akin to old school television, where the price we paid to watch our favorite sitcom was to suffer through the commercials. When we write a Gmail, post on Facebook, or create a Pinterest Board and then experience pervasive ads about that subject following us all over the Internet, we are simply participating in the modern information age of commercial advertising.

Targeted Internet advertising can be extremely powerful, and as we will cover in Chapter 19, you can leverage these powerful tools to grow your business. But that doesn't mean you should use free tools to run your business. As an entrepreneur, your business needs to be the attraction and not the audience. If you try to leverage these services by asking your clients to use them to connect with you, you will soon have your clients' attention being grabbed by other businesses advertising on the same platforms.

Even if that doesn't bother you much, the simple fact is that Google Calendar, Outlook 365, Square Scheduler, Wix Scheduler, and other generic calendaring tools aren't configured to help you run and grow your business. They won't enforce your appointment or class booking rules; won't connect payments to bookings; won't enable you to sell gift cards, memberships, or multi-session passes; won't let you manage appointment requests or waitlists; and won't help you keep your clients engaged.

The extra time you spend doing all of these things manually could cost you hundreds or even thousands of dollars per month in lost revenue and forever hold your business back. You'll soon feel like a hamster running as fast as you can on a wheel that is going nowhere. In short, trying to save money by using free or really inexpensive software tools could end up being one of the most expensive mistakes you ever make.

Software Buying Mistake #2: Trying to Develop Your Own Custom Solution

Note: If you have no intention of developing your own software, you can skip ahead. If you are entertaining the idea, please read this section carefully.

Suppose you have a differentiated wellness business model in mind. You've surveyed the market of software providers and none offer precisely what you are looking for. You have three alternative paths to choose:

1. Modify your business model to work with the existing readily available software.
2. Build a custom software app that integrates with an existing software platform via API ("application programming interface").
3. Build your own complete custom software.

For 99 percent of the people reading this book, you should take door number 1. For the other 1 percent, door number 2 might be a viable option. Absolutely no one should take door number 3. Trust me on this. Going down the custom software road is a house of pain, far more costly and difficult than most people can imagine.

Creating commercial-grade cloud software is hard. I know about hard things. I used to be a nuclear submarine officer. I was involved in nuclear energy and commercial space launch. Then I co-founded Mindbody in my garage and that is the hardest thing I have ever done.

If you embark on the path of developing your own software as a wellness business owner, you will need to devote hundreds of thousands or even millions of dollars to that project before the thing you build is even usable. Worse, you will waste years of precious time.

By the time you release that version 1, it will already be out of date. That's because none of us in the software business today are standing still, and the mobile operating systems and web browsers we are building to are constantly evolving. In three years, the product you and your team so lovingly designed and sweated over will feel like a twenty-year-old car, compared to the off-the-shelf products Mindbody and others will be offering for a few hundred dollars per month.

Then there are the bugs. In software, bugs are an unavoidable fact of life. The best software in the world developed for billions of dollars by the tech giants still has bugs. Do you think your custom application won't? Even if your software developers are geniuses capable of releasing perfect bug-free software, it won't stay that way. This is because the web browsers and smartphone operating systems your engineers will design to are themselves imperfect and constantly changing. Every time Apple, Microsoft, Facebook, or Google releases an update, your software will develop new bugs that you will have to fix.

Then there are the rapidly evolving regulatory requirements. If your application is dealing with people's private information, you will likely need to modify your application repeatedly in the years ahead to keep up with data privacy laws.

That is why the ultimate truth in any software platform is that it will never be done. Mindbody has been continuously building and innovating on its platform for more than two decades and is spending tens of millions of dollars per year just to keep it secure, up-to-date, and legally compliant. When you engage Mindbody as your software platform, for example, you get all of that for a few hundred dollars per month.

In the end, your reward for creating your own bespoke software will be to join companies like Mindbody in a perpetual innovation race, where the costs of ongoing development are continually rising and unending. Those folks who lived on pizza and Red Bull while they worked sixteen hours per day for three years to grind out your minimum viable product? They're making $250,000 per year working for Amazon, Google, or Facebook. Every time they pick up the phone to discuss your bug or feature request, they'll be billing you $200 per hour, if they even bother to pick up the phone at all. Software developers are the hottest commodities in the world right now, and they will be for decades to come.

If you have that kind of talent and energy to join that race, God bless you. You should start a software company, not a wellness business.

That leaves door number 2—the middle path. Mindbody and a few of its competitors have developed robust APIs that enable others to build applications on top of its platform. As of early 2020, there are over 800 authorized developers creating solutions on top of the Mindbody API. These range from custom reporting and marketing tools to mobile applications to hardware interfaces. Nearly 100 of those have graduated to being full-time Platform Partners, offering pre-built solutions you can purchase and implement with little or no customization required. This is a viable alternative, and I invite you to check out Mindbody's Platform Partner Ecosystem at https://marketplace.mindbodyonline.com/.

When to Implement Your Software and Payments Platform

The ideal time to implement your business's software platform is two to three months before your planned business launch date. Implementing earlier may leave you and your team rusty on how everything works by the time opening day rolls around, and waiting until the final few weeks before opening day will leave you and your team unnecessarily stressed at one of the most crucial periods in your business's history. In those significant final weeks before opening, you will need to be focused on finishing your buildout, training your staff, and promoting your soon-to-open business by pre-selling memberships and gift cards. Those activities will be enabled by your integrated software and payments platform.

Your software provider should include multiple hours of live consultative training in the software service agreement. This implementation support is typically delivered via web conferencing software. Many software providers such as Mindbody also offer premium onboarding options that enable you to delegate the setup work to a software expert while you focus on other aspects of your launch. If you can afford this additional premium service, I highly recommend it. Robust business management solutions like Mindbody are complex, and there is a considerable amount of work to be done to fully model your business in the platform.

However, if you are comfortable with cloud technologies, detail oriented, and on a tight budget, you can set up the software yourself with the help of your onboarding specialist. These are the most important steps you will need to complete 60–90 days before you open your doors:

- Set up your software options to model your class and appointment types and various scheduling and cancellation rules.
- Enter your menu of services, as well as various package and membership pricing options.
- Enter your team members and set up their software permissions, logins, qualifications, payroll amounts, and availabilities to perform different services.

- (If you are selling retail products) Enter your product SKUs, pricing, initial inventory on hand, and reorder points.
- Activate your merchant account processing so you can accept customer credit and debit cards at the front desk, on your website, and on mobile apps.
- Set up your point of sale hardware.
- Set up your listings on the Mindbody App and other business listing services. (See Chapter 17.)
- (If you opted into a branded mobile app) Apply for your DUNS Number and setup your Apple Developer and Google Play accounts. Then approve the design of your app and submit it to the iTunes and Google Play stores.

By carefully considering the capabilities you will need in your software platform, choosing a provider who will support and evolve with you, planning your software implementation at least two months in advance of opening, and fully leveraging your provider's coaching and consultation, you will minimize opening day stress on you and your team and maximize your revenue growth in the critical early months.

16 | Assemble Your Business Plan

We began this book by describing the process of making a living in wellness as a Hero's Journey: an extraordinary experience where the entrepreneur leaves the relative safety of a "normal" existence and enters a world of supernatural wonder. We later extended that metaphor by comparing the different types of wellness businesses one might choose to the six classes of white water rapids. A well written business plan completes the metaphor by imagining your hero's journey into the turbulent and exciting waters before you ever leave shore. Before we write the plan, let's go to the shores of that river where the adventure is about to begin.

After months of planning we assemble with our small group of fellow rafters along the banks of a beautiful river. We meet our river guide, who provides a quick safety briefing as we don life vests and climb into our boat. Everyone is given an oar and it quickly dawns on us that we are not simply passengers, but rather active participants in this journey, expected to row to ensure a successful outcome. We further realize that our river guide is in fact our captain on the water, as she takes the helm at the rear of the boat and begins to teach us how to respond to her commands and paddle in unison. Soon, we are comfortably maneuvering the boat forward and back, left and right under her orders in the relatively calm waters near the launch point. This "learn by doing" approach gives us a quiet sense of confidence as we take in the peaceful scenery and gorgeous canyon vistas. Our adventure is about to begin.

Eventually, we hear the distant roar of churning water downstream. Faint at first and growing steadily in intensity, that roar tells us that the rapids are quickly approaching. Our captain reminds us to hook in our feet under the seat in front of us to avoid getting tossed overboard as we tighten our grips on our paddles and prepare for the inevitable. Soon, the white water is upon us and all hell breaks loose. Our boat rapidly accelerates as it drops into the swirling rapids and our captain shouts urgent orders above the din. We paddle furiously to navigate around swirling, powerful water hazards and terrifying boulders.

Then, just as suddenly as it all began, our boat exits the rapids and that same water that appeared so threatening a few moments before returns to quiet peacefulness. As the roar recedes behind us, we let out defiant cheers, basking in a shared dopamine and serotonin rush of having triumphed over adversity and "survived" a harrowing experience together.

This is what you want your business launch to feel like. In this metaphor, the boat represents your business, the crew is your team, and you are the captain. If you have no team, then you are in the boat paddling alone. The safety briefing represents the staff training you will conduct before you launch your business, and the paddling practice represents the soft launch you will work into your plan, where you work the kinks out of your business before large numbers of customers engage.

Unlike our experienced white-water river guide, however, you've never done this before. You may have run rapids in other people's boats, but you've never been THE ONE ultimately responsible. To make the journey even more fraught, you are embarking on this journey for the first time in a custom boat that you conceived and designed that has never been in a real river before.

If someone gave you this impossible task, you would surely protest. This is insanity! Why are we even doing this?!

But suppose you had to do it. Suppose for whatever reason, you had no choice but to get into that boat and run it down that river. That's the reality of launching your wellness business. At some point, the time for planning and talking has passed. You have to put the boat in the water, climb into the damned thing, and push it away from the shoreline.

How does anyone maximize their chances for success in that scenario? In truth, this question is the entire reason I wrote this book. Across twenty years serving tens of thousands of wellness entrepreneurs like you, I have been privileged to witness some of the best-executed wellness business launches in history and have shared the pain of witnessing some of the worst. In truth, the vast majority of the launches we have seen at Mindbody fall somewhere in between these two extremes.

My intention in the chapters leading up to here has been to prepare you for the magic moment when you get into the boat that you built and push off from the safety of the shore. By absorbing this book and doing the thinking and exercises it calls for, you are nearly ready to do so.

But before you launch, you are going to write down your intentions in a clear and concise plan. This task is typically done in a "slide deck" using PowerPoint or Google Slides so that your deck of slides can be used in presentations and meetings. This plan is going to become your flag on the hill, the thing you can point to so that you and everyone engaged with you in this endeavor stays aligned and focused on a successful outcome in the journey ahead.

Why You Need a Business Plan Slide Deck

A business plan presentation prepared in PowerPoint or Google Slides is called your **deck**, a throwback term from the old days when people printed presentations onto translucent slides for use on an overhead projector. Entrepreneurs seeking capital to launch their business would prepare their deck of slides, stuff them in a briefcase, and carry them from meeting to meeting, pitching their business idea to skeptical bankers and prospective investors.

We still call these business plan presentations "decks" today, but the process of creating, sharing, and presenting them is much easier. You will create your deck in Microsoft PowerPoint or Google Slides and it may never be printed out. More often, you will email it to prospective lenders and investors. For those seriously interested, you may be asked to present it on a wall-mounted monitor or desktop projector.

If the idea of public speaking terrifies you, practice presenting your business plan with your mentor, family, or friends until you can deliver it without breaking into a cold sweat. It's worth the effort. The quality of these presentations and the ability of founders to stand up and deliver them to an audience is often the defining difference between getting the funding you need or not.

You must prepare one of these decks if you have a business partner and if you intend to ask others for money to fund your business. Even if neither of these scenarios apply, you should still prepare a business plan deck. The discipline of doing so will help to prevent you from skipping important steps in the creation of your business and give you a North Star reference to gaze at when your boat enters the rapids. And you will enter the rapids.

Fortunately, if you have done the preparation outlined in this book, the process of creating your business plan deck will be one of the easiest steps in your entrepreneurial journey. The deck should be succinct and should consist of no more than 10–12 slides.

The Perfect 10-Slide Deck

To understand the elements of the perfect business plan deck, let's stay in the white-water rafting metaphor a bit longer. How would you plan and prepare for the seemingly impossible task of navigating a potentially dangerous river as an inexperienced river guide in an untested boat? First, you and everyone involved would need to know why are doing this. If you don't know what lit the burning fire in your belly to build this boat and brave these waters, nobody will climb into that boat with you.

Business Plan Slide 1: Your Purpose Statement

Your first slide will include a simple recitation of your purpose statement, explaining your vision and mission for the business (see Chapter 13). When you present this slide, you will talk about what drew you to wellness in the first place, why you now feel compelled to start your own business, and how you are utterly committed to creating a successful business. Your audience needs to know that you will run through walls to see your own vision to fruition.

If I'm climbing into your boat with you, it's you that I'm betting on above all else. I probably don't know much about boats or river rafting. To convince me to support your adventure, you will need to describe how much you know about white-water rafting, with a particular focus on your multiple trips down the actual river we are embarking on.

Business Plan Slide 2: Your Industry Expertise

On your second slide, you will summarize the wellness industry expertise of you and your co-founders. This will include your relevant licenses and certifications, as well as your direct operating experience in the wellness market you are about to enter. When you present this slide, you will share a few anecdotes of your time in the industry, emphasizing how this experience has shaped your business vision.

To maximize your chances of success, you will have carefully studied and cataloged the most significant hazards in the river, those obstacles that can damage or flip over your boat, as well as your strategy for successfully maneuvering around them.

Business Plan Slide 3: Target Market Customers

On your third slide, you will include a summary of your market research, indicating that you understand your target market, their tastes, and their willingness to spend money on the products and services you will offer. When you present this slide, you will explain how you gained special insight into these particular types of consumers. You may be one of them, or you may have served them in your prior career. The key point you must make is that you have unique insight into your target market customers that others don't.

Business Plan Slide 4: Competition

This fourth slide about your competition will be the most complex to assemble, and it is utterly essential. Entrepreneurs who claim to have no competition are rarely funded, even if that unlikely statement is true on some level. A lack of competition implies that there is no proven market for the type of business you are creating, and that is perhaps the riskiest business startup of all.

Therefore, you will need to first identify in a separate document all of your relevant competitors, especially those you are confident you can beat with your target market customers. In this document, you will give a summary description of each, describing their services, pricing, target market focus, and perceived strengths and weaknesses. You will not present this document, but you will have it at the ready in case your prospective lenders or investors ask for it.

In your deck, you will summarize your competitive analysis in a 2x2 or 3x3 grid that highlights how your business is differentiated to prevail against your competition. Figure 16.1 shows a 3x3 grid for a hypothetical fitness studio. Your voiceover when presenting this slide would go something like this:

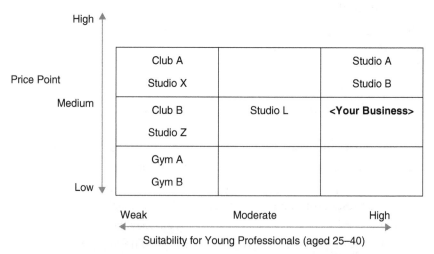

Figure 16.1   Example Competitor Matrix

As you can see, there are multiple businesses similar to ours in this market. However, most are not well suited for our target market of young professionals. Their experiences tend to either favor a college-aged crowd or older mid-career people. This is reflected in the décor, music, and workout programming.

Studio L is in our price point range and has made a half-hearted attempt to address our audience, but their studio design and most classes are still optimized for mid-career professionals. The young professionals they have managed to attract will find our experience much more appealing.

Lastly, Studios A and B are delivering a desirable wellness experience competitive with ours, but their prices are too high for many people. Our competitive price advantage will enable us to attract many of their customers as well.

In the rafting metaphor, given the nature of the river and hazards you face, you will outline the key features you have designed into your boat that make it well-suited to successfully navigate the river.

Business Plan Slide 5: Competitive Advantage

On your fifth slide, you will reiterate the voiceover you gave on slide 4, adding a bit more data and detail to explain how your differentiated experiences and cost structure will give your wellness business a competitive advantage over key competitors.

Business Plan Slide 6: Floorplan (for Retail Wellness) or Wireframes (for Virtual Wellness)

On your sixth slide, you will help the reader visualize your experience delivery model. If you are opening a brick-and-mortar business, a studio floor plan with a few sample photos of the experience dropped in will be highly effective. If you are creating a virtual wellness business, then simple wireframe mockups and screenshots of videos, as well as links to your YouTube Channel, will help bring your vision to life. In both cases, you will point out how this design is appealing to your target market customers.

Business Plan Slide 7: Menu of Services and Products

On your seventh slide, you will describe the main classes, appointment-based services, and related products you plan to sell. It is not necessary to list them all, just the major categories.

Business Plan Slide 8: Unit Economics

On your eighth slide, you will describe the different packages, bundles, and memberships you will offer and the resulting average price per service, cost of delivery, and gross margin you expect to yield for each service category.

Business Plan Slide 9: Financial Forecast

Based on your analysis in slide 8, you will create in your ninth slide a financial forecast of your first twelve months of operation and how much cash your business will burn before it achieves break even.

Business Plan Slide 10: Exit Strategy

Your tenth slide will deal with your exit strategy. Every wellness business plan should include one. How will you sell or shut down your business and pay off your debts? If you are raising money from others, how will they get paid back?

Tips on Creating and Delivering a Great Business Plan Presentation

PowerPoint and Google Slides are fabulous tools for focusing people's attention and conveying important information, providing you follow these simple rules:

- **Use Less Words and More Meaning.** Your business plan deck is a summary outline of the vast insights, knowledge, and planning you are bringing into your business. It does not need to include everything you know. In fact, few people have patience for that in today's world. Far better to select your most compelling and original ideas and convey those in short bullets, allowing the more nuanced depth of your knowledge to come through when you present the deck and answer people's questions.

- **Tell Your Story in the Title Boxes.** This simple trick will help steer your audience toward the most important conclusions and keep you focused when you present the deck. Use the title box at the top of each slide to simply state your intended message on that slide. Be sure these messages hold together into a simple and powerful narrative. For example, following the slide outline above, here's how the titles of the first five slides might read:
  - Slide 1: "An Inspiring Purpose That Unites Our Team"
  - Slide 2: "Founded by Wellness Industry Experts"
  - Slide 3: "Focused on the Tastes and Desires of <your target market>"
  - Slide 4: "Our Competition Has Left a Gap in the Market That We Will Fill"
  - Slide 5: "Our Technology Gives Us Competitive Advantage"
- **Be Sure Your Slides Are Readable.** Some of the worst presentations I have seen were written in small, lightly shaded fonts, where the presenter starts their presentation by saying, "This slide is a bit of an eye chart." Please don't ever say that. If your slides are "eye charts," then fix them before the presentation. As a good test, put your presentation on a projected screen or small laptop in a brightly lit room. Then have trusted friends or advisors stand back several feet and read each slide to you. If they struggle to read any of it, then reduce the number of words and improve your font sizes and colors until they can read it. Some of the best presentations I've seen are simply written in black and white.
- **Keep the Creative Design Spare and Authentic.** A few well-chosen graphics and authentic photos (not stock photography) depicting the wellness experiences you will deliver are good. An overproduced slide deck that uses a lot of distracting color or wastes valuable presentation space with repetitive graphics is bad. You need room to keep your font sizes as large as possible. You want your audience focused on the power of your ideas and the depth of your preparation, not on the visual complexity of the slide.

That's it. You've done it! Assembling a business plan is hard and necessary work that will help keep you and your team on track and help you secure your financing.

PART V

Launch Your Business

17

Launch Your Website and Establish Your Online Presence

With your preparatory work in Parts III and IV completed, you are ready now to set up your website and establish an online presence for your business. Doing so is easy, inexpensive, and utterly essential to secure the financing you will need to launch your business. Even if you don't need additional financing to launch, completing the steps covered in this chapter at least two months before you plan to deliver your first wellness class or appointment will give you early visibility and make your launch far more successful.

Understanding Marketing

When business owners "market" their businesses, they are taking conscious action to attract new clients and keep them coming back. **Marketing** is the science and art of doing that, and the good news for small business owners is that the most effective marketing techniques available to them today are inexpensive or free. Conversely, paid advertising and influencers are far more expensive, and you will likely need to use them as well. We will cover that topic fully in Chapter 19, but before you spend your first dollar on advertising, you will want to set your business up for early success by fully leveraging the free and low-cost techniques covered in this chapter. This is why it is so important to understand and map out your marketing strategy before you build your website.

Focus on Your Target Market

In Chapter 10, you profiled the types of people you have designed your business around. You know these people—what they like, where they live, what they have, and what they lack. These factors are the defining difference between an online presence that pops and sizzles and one that few people notice. Your target market must notice you. Whoever said "there is no such thing as bad publicity" has clearly been proven wrong by the events of the twenty-first century. But the underlying point that publicity is important stands true. Individuals in your target market cannot choose your business unless they know that you exist. And after they notice that you exist, you need to deliver a message that attracts them to you. To do that reliably and predictably, you need to develop your *customer personas*.

Define Your Customer Personas

Customer personas are not real people. They are fictional archetypes representing the key traits of the hundreds or even thousands of people you want to attract into your business. Defining these archetypes is useful because it gives you easy-to-reference profiles you and your team can refer back to repeatedly in the months ahead. You will be able to quickly answer the ultimate question in any marketing activity: "Will this website/Facebook page/Instagram site/ad attract this kind of person?"

The best customer personas give insight into how real people in your target market weigh options and make buying decisions, enabling you to craft marketing elements and campaigns that effectively attract real people like them into your business. Most wellness businesses need two or three personas. There are myriad ways to describe or depict your personas and there are multiple free online tools to help you do so. These are the best:

https://www.hubspot.com/make-my-persona

https://xtensio.com/user-persona/

https://www.socialbakers.com/free-social-tools/create-your-persona

Here are two example personas to give you the basic idea:

John is a 57-year-old college professor at the local university. He knows the importance of exercise, but has trouble staying motivated. He owns a smartphone but rarely uses more than a few basic functions. He prefers to visit websites and search for things from his home or work PC, and he rarely books his classes or appointments online, preferring instead to speak to someone on the phone.

Leigh is a 34-year-old sales executive who works long hours and travels frequently for business. She was an athlete in college, but now only exercises sporadically. Leigh wants to lose weight and rebuild the strength and agility she had in college. She does everything on her phone and she wouldn't go to a wellness business unless she could find the business and book appointments from her phone.

Before you create your website, you'll want to create three or four personas like this, which collectively define your **target market**. And you'll want to print them out and display them prominently in your private office or wherever you work on your marketing activities. Seeing them daily will help focus and inspire everything you do in your business—and it will prompt you to refresh and update these personas when needed. Once you have your client personas in place, you can craft the visuals and messaging on your website to appeal to them.

Set Up Your Website

The first thing to remember about your website is that it is a cornerstone of your online presence. Some will say in the age of powerful online tools outlined in the next section that a very small wellness business doesn't need a website. I disagree. The other online tools are important, but all of them should drive more people to your website. Your website is the cornerstone of your brand and online presence, and the more traffic it receives, the more valuable all of that becomes.

Fortunately, building a great website has never been easier or less expensive. Powerful website platforms such as www.weebly.com, www.wix.com, www.squarespace.com, and www.godaddy.com offer very useful templates and content management systems that integrate with your online booking and payments platform and enable you to manage your own site without a web developer.

Each of these web content management providers has excellent online tools and tutorials, including important guidelines on *search engine optimization* (SEO). Here are some guidelines specific to wellness businesses:

- **Keep it simple.** Nobody wants to read thick paragraphs online. The best websites are like the best presentations. They are spare in their language and use high-contrast, large fonts that are pleasing to look at and easy to read.
- **Conform to established norms.** Through thousands of website visits per year, we have all developed a subconscious muscle memory of where to look for navigation bars, pull-down menus, and other common elements. Those norms are built into the best website templates provided by the leading content management systems. Use those and resist the urge to be original in your site layout. Your website is the cornerstone of your business marketing strategy, not the zenith of your creative expression.
- **Leverage clear and compelling calls to actions (CTAs).** The point of your website is to compel target market clients into action. You want them to "Book Now," "Buy Gift Cards," "Try Our Intro Offer," or "Join Our Mailing List." So say it. Don't be subtle.
- **Keep online booking and purchasing never more than one click away.** In fact, there should be multiple paths in your website that lead people to online booking and purchasing. This "All Paths Lead to Rome" approach will ensure you don't lose anyone who is truly interested.
- **Sell gift cards.** These cause clients to refer others to something they enjoy, and your business gets an interest-free cash advance on that future product or service.
- **Have dedicated pages for pricing, introductory offers, and membership.** These will ensure that the search engines pick them up.
- **Include high-quality photos and bios of you and your team.** Wellness is personal and the most important question people have before they book a class or service is who will be providing it.
- **Make your introductory offers truly compelling.** The best offers are long enough to create a habit and inexpensive enough to be an easy upsell off of a drop-in single session; for example, "Two weeks of unlimited classes for $30" or "Three massages for the price of two."
- **Include a video tour of your business and video testimonials from happy clients.** You can do this easily by recording your videos

on Instagram, or uploading them to YouTube, and linking those to your site.

- **Verify after every update that your website is still "mobile responsive."** Your web pages should automatically resize and reorient for optimal viewing on tablets and mobile phones. You do this simply by resizing your web browser window on your screen or by pulling up your site on a tablet and phone and navigating through all the screens. All of the leading website providers have mobile-responsive templates, but you will need to follow their instructions when you upload photos or graphical elements to ensure you don't break that responsiveness.
- **Verify after every update that your website still loads fast.** Most web CMS platforms have this figured out, automatically resizing photos for optimal screen load. But you need to confirm it. Clear the cache on your web browser and click reload. It should take no more than three seconds for your site to fully load on your browser. If it takes longer, then start cutting back graphics and reducing the size of your photos until your site is fast. Better that it has spare graphics and loads fast—even in an area with weak mobile service—than have spectacular graphics and take too long.

Activate Your Free Online Business Listings

Multiple paid advertising platforms are available for small businesses today, and we will talk about them in Chapter 19. For now, before you pull together your business plan, look for money to finance your launch, or spend your first dollar on advertising, you need to fully leverage the free business listings that are available to you.

Free Search Engine Listings

Search engines enable people to find things on the Internet. Since the dawn of the Internet there have been dozens of search engines, but outside of Russia and China, there are only two that matter today: Google and Microsoft Bing. Here's how to make sure your business is beautifully represented in both without spending a dime.

Google My Business

A Google My Business listing enables people searching across all Google products, including Maps, Search, and Local, to see a compelling view of your wellness business with photos, descriptions, a menu of classes and services, and a live bookable schedule, providing you are using a Google integrated business management software. This service also includes a powerful reviews engine that consumers are increasingly relying on. The reviews will be automatically created by your clients once you are open for business, but the rest of the content must be uploaded and managed by you—and it's easy to do.

Open up any web browser, search for "Google My Business," and follow the instructions to claim your business and complete your listing. Then put a quarterly reminder in whatever calendaring tool you use to update your listing at least every quarter.

Bing Places for Business

Places for Business is a free Bing service that enables businesses to add their business listings to Microsoft Bing searches. While not nearly as popular as Google, there are still hundreds of millions of searches per month on Bing, so you should do this. The process to claim your business and set up your listing is very similar to Google My Business and you can reuse the same content for both. Just search for it on any browser to be taken to a simple online form to do so.

Free Social Media Listings

The term *social media* defines the websites and mobile apps that enable billions of people to create and share content or network with each other. There are hundreds of active social media sites today, and the most popular are names we all know well, including Facebook, Instagram, YouTube, and Twitter.

Facebook Page

In the world of Facebook, *profiles* are for people and *pages* are for businesses. Regardless of how you feel about the most popular social network in the world, whether you feel that Facebook is a wonderful tool, a nuisance, or a threat to democracy, this is your moment to set those thoughts aside and leverage this powerful platform to fuel your business. Facebook has nearly two billion daily active users, and 74 percent of them are in high-income households.

In addition to driving more people to your website, your Facebook page will give you an easy way to build social media followers and humanize your brand by uploading a steady stream of fresh content, including updates on your business and photos or videos of recent events. This will keep you closely connected with new and existing clients alike.

Many ways exist to build a community on your Facebook page so that it turns into a hub for current and potential clients to provide feedback, reviews, and engagement with your brand. These include:

- Organizing contests or promotions
- Prompting your followers with engaging questions
- Providing a place to leave reviews
- Offering incentives for sharing your content
- Posting relevant articles and material

You can also think of your Facebook page followers as participants in an ongoing focus group. Through their interactions with your content, you can poll their feelings about your business, measure their interest level in new ideas, and gauge their sentiment about your business overall.

In short, a Facebook page is essential for any wellness business. It lays the groundwork for highly effective advertising campaigns down the road and it is free. So log into www.facebook.com and set up your Facebook page today!

Instagram Business Profile

Instagram is an extension of Facebook, with an emphasis on visual content, which can be helpful for business and advertising. By setting up an Instagram business profile you will provide another channel for clients to interact with your business and share their enthusiasm with their family and friends.

An Instagram business profile groups your business by industry, gives viewers a quick way to find your website and physical business address, and enables an instant Connect button right on the profile so that you quickly build followers. Your business profile also gives other Instagram users a chance to "tag" your business in their posts, which becomes an instant referral mechanism for their followers. You can then share the posts that you've been tagged in back to your own followers, creating a compounding followership for your brand.

Your Instagram business profile includes a powerful direct messaging feature, providing a great way to communicate with clients as well as other business owners and practitioners in your market. Instagram can catapult your client and community engagement and help drive more people to your website or mobile app listings for booking and purchasing.

YouTube Channel

Anyone can set up a YouTube Channel, and social media celebrities with the ability to generate hundreds of thousands of followers and millions of video watchers can generate a meaningful income by enrolling in Google's AdSense program, where you are paid for the advertising impressions your YouTube channel generates. But this is extremely hard to do—unless you are already famous. For the rest of us mere mortals, YouTube is a place to upload and store videos that you want to share with the world for free. If you anticipate assembling a substantial library of informational or promotional videos that you want to share with the general public, YouTube is the place to do it. However, if you want to create a library of on-demand videos that only paying members can access, you will need a business management integrated system like Mindbody's Virtual Wellness Platform.

Twitter

Twitter is an excellent platform to share your expertise, wisdom, and passion for your craft (in 280 characters or less). If you are someone who reads and writes a lot, Twitter can work well in conjunction with Facebook and Instagram to increase your brand awareness and build followers. These three platforms can be set to automatically repost anything on one into the other two. However, if you are more of a visual learner and verbal communicator you may find that Facebook and Instagram are sufficient to connect to your audience.

Yelp Page

Yelp is basically the modern-day Yellow Pages. It offers businesses the opportunity to attract new customers by reaching users who are actively looking for their category of businesses. Business owners can easily manage their Yelp page by adding photos, customizing their online storefront, adding important information like hours and services, and responding to customers who write reviews.

The Mindbody App

The Mindbody app connects your business to millions of consumers worldwide who actively engage in fitness, integrative health, spa, and salon services. By aggregating more than 2.5 million available wellness class and appointment sessions per day and offering powerful consumer friendly features such as instant Search, Favorites, Waitlists, Promoted Introductory Offers, and Last Minute Offers, and by providing the largest authentic consumer reviews platform in the industry, the Mindbody App is uniquely capable of attracting new clients to your business and keeping them coming back.

A Mindbody App listing is available free of charge to all businesses running on Mindbody or Booker business management software. You can upload and manage photos and descriptions of your business as well as list your amenities inside of your business management software.

18 | Secure Your Financing

Technology businesses, and especially cloud software companies, require an enormous amount of invested capital to grow, and over the past twenty years I have experienced every stage of business financing: from "bootstrapping" the startup with my wife's and my life savings and a second mortgage, to getting several hundred thousand dollars from friends and family when we desperately needed it two years later, to raising over $2 million from angel investors, to then raising more than $90 million in multiple private financing rounds from New York and Silicon Valley venture capitalists.

We took Mindbody public in 2015, raising over $400 million in the public markets before taking the company private again in 2019 with an acquisition by Vista Equity Partners for $1.9 billion. No, that doesn't make me a billionaire. Far from it. But as an entrepreneur it gives me great pleasure to know that the thousands of investors and employees who believed in us made large returns on their investments and after many years of living at or near the precipice of financial ruin, my family and I don't have to worry about money anymore.

Wellness businesses don't require as much cash as technology startups, but they are still economic engines and money – or "capital" – is the fuel they run on. It takes far more of this fuel to successfully launch a wellness business than most people imagine. This is true for the simple reason that you must build the engine that delivers the experiences that people will pay for before the first dollar of revenue can be earned and long before any profits are realized. For most wellness businesses it takes a year or more of planning and building before that first dollar is earned and another year before you can generate enough gross margin to cover your operating expenses (see Chapter 7).

The amount of capital you need to have on hand to sufficiently finance your business varies widely. You and your accountant or business consultant should create a spreadsheet to carefully tally your actual expected costs by month for a full two years (covering the twelve months before your business launches and a full year of operation thereafter). Be sure to include the following:

1. Attorney, accountant, and consultant fees
2. Business license fees
3. State LLC or incorporation fees
4. Website and technology platform startup and monthly subscription fees
5. Construction of tenant improvements (for a retail business)
6. Equipment and supplies
7. Twelve months of operating expenses
8. Cash reserves of at least three additional months of operating expenses after the business is reliably cash flow positive
9. Sufficient personal cash reserves to cover your own living expenses until the business can afford to pay you

Then, after all that, add a cushion of another 10% to your total cash requirements for the "oh s . . ." moments that will inevitably occur. In business, it is far better to have more cash than you need.

For most non-home-based wellness businesses in the United States, your total startup costs will be somewhere in the range of $300,000 to $600,000. It is possible for a very lean wellness business startup in a lower-cost city to be completed for less than $200,000, and it is not uncommon for premium wellness business startups in New York City, San Francisco, and London to exceed $800,000.

Even if you and your partners have access to that much money, I strongly urge you to seek at least a portion of your business financing from outside sources before risking most or all of your own nest eggs. Even with the most careful preparations, a startup business comes with inherent risk and success is never guaranteed.

Three categories of business financing are available to most wellness businesses: friends and family, commercial banks, and private investors.

Friends and Family Financing

For many people, loved ones with money are the most accessible source of capital to start a business. It makes sense. These are the people we love and trust the most and with whom we share close personal bonds. These are also the people most likely to wish us success and happiness in our lives. This is why nearly every startup I am aware of began with at least a component of "friends and family" money.

In my entrepreneurial journey, I have had the good fortune of being on the receiving end of these arrangements multiple times, co-founding Mindbody with loans and equity investments from my parents, brothers, and a few friends. More recently, I have been on the giving side of friends and family financing as well, contributing a significant portion of the cash needed to help my nephew, wife, and son start their own businesses.

Most of my arrangements went well, but a few did not. One resulted in a painful lawsuit and a lost friendship rift that took more than a decade to heal. From that broad spectrum of experiences, I pass along three hard-won lessons:

Friends and Family Lesson #1: Ensure they know what they are getting into.

Insist on presenting your wellness business plan to your loved ones before they decide whether or not to back you. This will help them clearly understand your intentions and appreciate the deep effort and thought you have put into your business. It will also remind them that all business startups are risky. If losing the money they are about to hand over to you would be painful, they should not write the check.

Friends and Family Lesson #2: A borrower or a lender be, not a partner.

Unless the friends or family members are going to be operationally involved in your business, they should be your lender, not your equity investor. The difference is profound.

Lenders have no operational voice in your business and no liability when something goes wrong. They get paid back with interest according to an agreed upon schedule, regardless of how well the business does.

An equity investor, on the other hand, becomes your partner. Their financial outcome is tied to the success of your business and in some cases they could even become personally liable as well. With all that responsibility comes rights, and your loved one who invested in your business may soon gain a voice in your business. They will likely want to read periodic financial reports and may even wish to observe board and management meetings. Equity investing in startups is an adventure suitable for experienced investment professionals, not your grandparents.

Some would argue that investors are better than lenders because you don't have to make payments back to them in the early life of the business. If your business fails, the value of their investment goes to zero along with yours. In that scenario, you never have to pay them back.

For these reasons the investor arrangement may sound appealing. But take a moment and consider how it would feel with friends and family. Having your parents or close friends involved in your business could put a strain on your relationship. In the event of business failure, the reality of never paying them back could create a rift in the family or permanently damage a dear friendship. If you are fortunate enough to have a loved one handing you money they don't expect to have paid back, then accept it as a gift and document it accordingly for tax reasons. Otherwise, treat their money as a loan that you fully expect to pay back with interest—even if your business fails.

Friends and Family Lesson #3: Get it in writing.

You are a businessperson now. Every transference of money between you, your business, and someone else should be documented in writing—a check with the intention of the funds noted in the memo and a receipt confirming acceptance of the money in writing.

In the case of a business loan, your attorney needs to draft up a bona fide promissory note and you should encourage your loved one to have their own attorney review it. These agreements will precisely outline the term of the financing, interest rate, method and timing of payments, and any other expectations between the borrower and lender. Family money often comes with strings attached, and if Grandma Mary expects you to rent her building, give a job to your cousin Jimmy, or come to Sunday dinners, all of those expectations should be documented in your loan agreement.

All of this may sound like overkill, but trust me on this. Written agreements and lawyers are essential in business because we human beings are imperfect. Ever play the game of telephone? Two people can be in the same conversation and hear two completely different things. Even if they both understood what was said, one or both may soon forget or develop a divergent memory of that conversation. This is especially true when the agreements were made in an atmosphere of love and trust, and the stresses of business later puts strain on the relationship.

Remember what I said about lawyers in Chapter 9? They are like dentists. You will either pay a small amount for preventive care now or face costly and painful root canals later.

In the end, just remember that mixing business and personal relationships introduces a special level of risk to both. Unfortunately, for most entrepreneurs, friends and family money may be the only viable source of financing in the early stages of the business.

Commercial Bank Financing

Shortly after Mindbody's launch, my dad conveyed a simple truth he had learned in his forty years of small business ownership: "The bank will only loan you money if you can prove you don't need it." His words proved prophetic. Other than the second mortgage on my home that funded Mindbody's launch, which I was able to obtain only because I still had a good paying job outside of the business, my co-founders and I were unable to secure bank financing until long after Mindbody had grown to several million dollars in annual revenue. Even then, we were able to secure only a very small business line of credit. In short, my co-founders and I were able to borrow money from a bank only after we proved that Mindbody no longer needed it. We secured that line of credit regardless, because we knew that life and business are unpredictable.

Even though that business line of credit was small at first, and we had plenty of cash in the bank at the time, we deliberately dipped into the line and paid if off repeatedly. Thus we used the line of credit to increase our working capital and build creditworthiness in the eyes of the bank. As our business grew, our bank gradually increased our credit line from the starting number of $150,000 to $1 million. Later, when Mindbody became a large business, we were able to transfer that banking relationship to a more substantial institution, leveraging our perfect payment record to secure a credit line of $10 million.

But all of that is down the road for you. In the months leading up to the launch of your business, it would be easier to borrow $100,000 to purchase an expensive automobile (don't do it!) than it would be to borrow the same amount to fund your business. This is because auto loans are collateralized by the vehicle you are purchasing. If you were unable to continue making payments, the bank can repossess the vehicle to recover the remaining balance of the loan. With a small business, on the other hand, if the entrepreneur is no longer able to make her payments, the underlying business she used to collateralize the loan would likely be worthless to the bank. In the rare cases where small business loans are funded, it is usually when the business owner personally guarantees the note, has a friend or family member with high net worth co-sign the note, or pledges some "hard asset" such as their home as collateral.

If you choose to use your home or other piece of real estate as collateral for a business loan, you must remember this means the bank will take your home from you if your business loan defaults. This happened to my parents in the early 1990s. They had pledged their home as collateral for a business loan to expand their retail lighting store. When their business was hit hard by a deep recession a few years later, they soon found themselves no longer able to keep up with their business loan payments, and the bank repossessed the house they had owned for nearly thirty years. It didn't matter that the remaining principal balance was a tiny fraction of what the home was worth and that they had never missed a mortgage payment. The bank took their home anyway. Rather than pledging your home as collateral, it would be far better to refinance it and use a portion of those proceeds to finance your business.

In several countries, there are government-backed lending programs designed to support small business formation. In the United States, this includes the Small Business Administration loan guarantee program—commonly referred to as an "SBA Guaranteed Loan." This is where the government guarantees the loan that a commercial bank makes to a small business, making it easier for the small business to qualify for financing. This might make sense for you, and a quick Google search will uncover dozens of online banks that will take your application.

Before you proceed in this direction, however, understand that it's the lender receiving the protection of the government guarantee, not the borrower. The loan is still originating from a commercial bank, which may still require you to personally guarantee your loan, pledge your hard assets, or seek a co-signer. If your business is subsequently unable to service the debt, the only entity being protected by the government is the bank. In fact, my parents' business loan was an SBA Guaranteed Loan. The SBA regulations actually required the bank to repossess my parents' home before they would cover any losses from the loan.

Private Equity Investors

Private equity firms manage and invest committed money from wealthy individuals, families, pension funds, and sovereign wealth funds. They make dozens or even hundreds of investments into businesses that hold promise of very high returns on their investment. This category of business financing has seen explosive growth over the past decade and is now a credible opportunity for many wellness businesses. Private equity can be categorized as shown in the following table.

INVESTOR TYPE	TYPICAL INVESTMENT FOCUS	DEFINING CHARACTERISTICS	INVESTMENT SIZES
Angel	Pre-revenue or minimal revenue startups with high growth potential	Motivated by both altruism and profit	$100K–$2M
Early Stage Venture Capital ("VC")	Startups with proven but still small revenue streams with high growth potential	Looking for breakthrough companies	$1M–$20M
Late Stage VC	Large revenue streams with high growth potential and probability of future IPO or acquisition	Looking for proven business models and teams	$20M–$100M
Growth-Oriented Private Equity ("PE")	Established growth businesses with a high prospect for continued strong growth and profitability	Looking for market leaders who need a tune-up	$20M–$2B
Cash Flow–Oriented PE	Mature businesses with slow growth and the prospect for high profit margins	Looking for "cash cows" with a very stable customer base	$5M–$100M

Within each of these categories are hundreds of PE/VC firms, each with their own distinct investment thesis, culture, and area of focus. And new ones are popping up all the time. While the personalities of PE/VC firms vary widely, you can count on all of them to have these traits in common:

1. They will all require you to form a C-corporation before accepting their invested capital. If you are seriously considering PE or VC investors down the road, you should form your business as a C-corporation incorporated in the State of Delaware, regardless of where you plan to operate your business.
2. They are all looking for exceptional returns on their investment—typically three to five times ("3–5X") their investment in three to five years.
3. They consider themselves to be experts in creating business value, will require regular reports from you, and will demand an active role on your board of directors.
4. If they are an Angel Group or VC, they will want a 10–20 percent equity ownership stake in your business and numerous "protective provisions" that will enable them to receive their money back before you or any earlier investor. They will want to limit how much money you can spend without their approval and will want veto rights over big decisions like selling your company.
5. If they are a classic PE firm, they will want a controlling stake in your business or will want to own your business outright. In either case, as CEO you effectively become an employee of the PE firm and can be fired at any time.

This is a lot to absorb and it's just scratching the surface. There is much more you need to know before you accept an equity investment from a private equity or venture capital firm. You should do so only under the active advice of an experienced attorney who has negotiated these deals before.

When it comes to finding funding for your wellness business, you should use your head, heart, and gut before making the final decision. If something about a financial deal makes you uncomfortable or just doesn't feel right to you, walk away. In the end this is your business and your dream. You should never take a deal that makes you uneasy.

19

Grow Your Clientele with Paid Marketing That Works

The Mindbody Team and I have been studying brick-and-mortar wellness businesses for more than two decades, and through all those years two hard and important facts have remained consistently true:

1. **You will always have room for more clients.** The average wellness business fills less than half of its available class or appointment spots per day.
2. **You will always need to bring in new clients.** The average wellness business needs to replace about half of its loyal clientele each year.

Highly successful wellness businesses do better in both of these metrics, and by carefully following the guidelines in this book your business will hopefully be among those. But even if you are filling two-thirds of your class and appointment spaces and only losing one-third of your loyal clients per year, and even if you have a strong online presence and are leveraging effective marketing techniques fully, you will still need a substantial paid advertising budget.

In fact, in the startup phase when growing your business and clientele is most urgent, you should plan on devoting about 20 percent of your early revenue goal to paid advertising. After your business has become sustainably profitable, you can reduce that investment to about 10 percent of revenue.

Before you activate the advertising and promotional methods described in this chapter, be sure you complete a review of Chapter 17.

Search Engine Marketing (SEM)

A successful **search engine marketing** (SEM) strategy involves three components: keyword phrases, the content of your ad, and your advertising budget.

Keyword phrases are the first component of a successful SEM strategy They connect the search terms consumers type into web browsers, maps, or mobile app windows when they are trying to find something related to the businesses that want to attract those consumers. It's important to remember that Google Adwords® and Microsoft Ads® will show your ad only when someone within the geographic area you have specified types in a search that includes one of your keyword phrases. Here are some examples you will want to use:

<your business type> <your city name>
Best <your business type> <your city name>
<your wellness discipline> <your city name>
Best <your wellness discipline> <your city name>
Best <your wellness discipline> near me

The second component of a successful SEM strategy is the content of your ad. Unlike digital display ads, which usually include special fonts, colors, photos, and even video, Google Adwords® and Microsoft Ads® return only a limited number of text words. Those few words are your call to action, and they need to be compelling and different enough from the many other ads likely to appear to capture the consumer's attention and cause them to click on them—so these words really matter!

This is where your intimate knowledge of your target market clients and the personas you developed in Chapter 17 come in handy. When you craft your ads, you will think about the words and phrasing likely to capture the attention of your personas. And you will want to experiment with different approaches to see which create the most clicks.

The third component of a successful SEM strategy is your advertising budget. You will pay for SEM ads only when people click on them; both Google Adwords® and Microsoft Ads® enable you to set the maximum amount you are willing to pay for a click and the maximum amount you will spend per month. You will want to start small with a total advertising budget of a few hundred dollars and a maximum cost per click of $5, and then work up from there.

Tracking Results of Your SEM

You will want to try **A/B Testing** in which you test a number of variations of an ad to determine which one performs better. When creating your ads, create two versions. Publish them and allow them to work for a few weeks. Then take a look to see which one performed better and then turn the other one off. You can measure the performance several ways, including CPM, CPC, and CTR:

- **Cost per Impression (CPM):** The rate you pay when your ad is shown per one thousand impressions. For the search ads we are talking about here, the impressions cost nothing. But seeing your CPM will give you an understanding of how many people in your region are searching for the keywords you set up.
- **Cost per Click (CPC):** The rate you pay when someone clicks on your ad, which varies according to the maximum amount you told the search engine that you would pay for that click and your SEO ranking for that search term. The more popular the search term, the more you are likely to pay. The better your SEO ranking for that search term, the less you are likely to pay.
- **CTR (Click-Through Rate):** The number of clicks that your ad receives divided by the number of impressions it receives. The average CTR for a search ad is about 2 percent and a good CTR is 4 percent, meaning for every 100 people who see your search ad, you can expect two to four people to click on it (https://blog.hubspot.com/agency/google-adwords-benchmark-data).

Advertising on Facebook

Facebook is one of the most effective advertising platforms you can leverage, because it has capabilities that the search engines do not. When people search for something on the Internet, they may spend a minute or less on Google or Microsoft Bing. But when they go on Facebook, they may be there for 30 minutes or more. More than 74 percent of Facebook users are high-income earners and Facebook's advertising features allow you to target people in ways that Google cannot. For example, you can upload an email list of your existing clientele or of people you know who fit your target market personas, and Facebook will create a lookalike audience for your ads on the Facebook platform. This vastly increases the odds that the people who see your ad on Facebook are likely to become good clients.

People who respond to your Facebook ads are likely to see the rich content and client interactions on your Facebook page and to read your Facebook reviews before they click through to your website.

The highest user traffic on Facebook occurs midday Wednesday and Thursday, which makes these times ideal to promote your business.

Tracking Results on Facebook

When you create a new Facebook Ad Campaign, the platform will ask you whether your objective is awareness, consideration, or conversion. *Awareness* means that you want people to become aware of your brand, your location, or your service offerings. *Consideration* means that you are looking for people to access your website, engage with your business online or in person, or complete a form or download something. *Conversion* means that you want the person to buy something or visit your business.

Conversion is the obvious objective for most wellness business owners, but awareness and consideration are important as well. When you build awareness for your business and when you drive more people to your website, you have the opportunity to convert them into paying customers later. Facebook has an array of powerful analytics tools that can help you track all of that. These systems are constantly evolving and improving, and they come with online tutorials. So think about your objectives; then log in and learn by doing.

Promoting Your Business with Influencers

Wellness businesses inspire passion in people, and many people speak about them daily. Some of these people have notable numbers of followers, and their words and advocacy can have a meaningful impact on your business. Your work with influencers may be as simple as asking clients who have enjoyed the classes or services you offer to post their endorsements on social media. The next step is to leverage an influencer marketing platform, such as www.upfluence.com, www.shopinshout.com, www.aspireiq.com, and www.captiv8.io, all of which have starter packages within reach for small wellness businesses.

Several kinds of influencers can have a tremendous impact on the success of your business:

- **Nano-Influencers.** These are people with a very small number of followers, but they have expertise in a highly specialized area. This might be one of your staff members who has a specific training and may have a following because he is very immersed in a given modality. Or it might be a customer who loves what you do and has a large group of like-minded friends that she connects with frequently.
- **Micro-Influencers.** These people are devoted to a specialized field or particular niche and have gained a sizable social media following among other devotees. Micro-influencers typically have between 1,000 and 40,000 followers. Over the past few years, more micro-influencers have gained recognition and have become increasingly famous for their online presence.
- **Macro-Influencers.** Macro-influencers are one step down from the mega-influencers. They may be more accessible as influencer marketers as they likely have a following of more than 40,000 but are not near the one million mark. Often these are up-and-coming celebrities or online experts who are willing to work with multiple brands.
- **Mega-Influencers.** These people have a vast number of followers on their social networks, commonly over one million followers. They have most likely hit celebrity status and will work with only large brands. They are paid high sums to use their influence publicly.

As you plan your work with influencers, start first by asking yourself these questions:

1. Which influencers are aligned with the core values of my business?
2. Which of these influencers has the largest following?
3. What does the influencer have to gain by working with me?
4. What am I looking to gain by partnering with the influencer?
5. How will I measure success?

Only when you have a clear understanding of the answers to these questions should you reach out to determine which influencers are open to partnering with your business.

Email Marketing

As you build your clientele, you will begin building a sizable email list and sharing a newsletter to keep your customers aware of any changes to your business as well as information to keep them focused on their health and well-being. Keep in mind that you will need to regularly focus on building content as well as attending to your Key Performance Indicators (KPIs), like open rates and bounce rates, to determine that you are offering your customers the right kind of content.

When building email marketing content, you should do the following:

- Create surveys to encourage customers to engage with you.
- Frequently adapt email content to customer interest and habits, and mention the customers who engage with you in your emails.
- Simplify emails so they are easily readable, and keep in-depth content on your website or blog.
- Tell customers how to engage on your social media platforms. Often they will do the shout-outs for you and influence others to engage more.
- Feature specific customers to show their stories and perhaps their results.
- Have contests and allow customers to win prizes.
- Have guest bloggers focus on a topic that is not your expertise—for example, nutrition, alternative medicine, or stress reduction.

You are going to need to do your best to get the results you are look-ing for from email marketing. And for that, *consistency* is key. If you always send a Tuesday email, then customers will expect it and look for it. Make sure that your headline is interesting and habit forming—for example, "Fit-ness Fridays" or "Wellness Wednesday Motivation." Always use professional images—it just doesn't pay to cut corners and there are so many great plat-forms that do this well. In addition, be sure to send emails from the same email address so they are easy to find.

Tracking Results of Your Email Marketing

Your email is only as good as its **open rate**. Your open rate is determined by the number of people who opened the email divided by the number of people who received the email. The average open rate across all industries is approximately 21 percent (https://mailchimp.com/resources/email-marketing-benchmarks/).

Opening an email is important, but it's far more important that you know who is actually clicking on your calls to action and following up with them. Spend the most time figuring out what is causing a good click-through rate (CTR). The CTR for email is determined by the percentage of people who clicked on at least one link in your email message divided by the number of people who received the email. According to Mail Chimp, the average click-through rate across all industries is 2.6 percent. Figure out how to increase the number of click-throughs. This is your mission.

Spend a little time on your bounce rates and unsubscribe rates. There will always be some errors in the process of email marketing. If you see a high bounce rate, you may want to check for spelling errors in your database. If you see high unsubscribe rates, you may want to adjust your messaging.

Non-Traditional Marketing

Gift Cards

It may not be obvious that gift cards are an amazing marketing tool. But think of it this way: gift card purchasers are your best customers by far.

These are people who have either received your services and loved their experience so much that they are willing to purchase them for someone else, or they have heard of your reputation and are so impressed, they are willing to purchase your services for someone else. The way that the gift card holder is treated must be paramount, and the customer who purchased the gift card should be treated like gold.

Podcasts

Many wellness professionals are beginning to look at podcasts as a vehicle for espousing their theories, methods, and wisdom. A podcast is a digital audio episode or series of episodes made available on the Internet to be streamed or available for download to a computer or mobile device. Again, this is the perfect avenue for projecting your image and literally your voice as a thought leader in your community and within your industry. There are multiple platforms that you can use to publish your podcast and get it in front of the right listeners. They include Apple Podcasts, Google Podcasts, Spotify, Stitcher, TuneIn, and SoundCloud.

Nine Tips for Better Marketing

Here are some recommendations from the Mindbody Marketing Team to improve your marketing efforts:

1. Practice consistency and patience. Occasional marketing doesn't work. If your clients only occasionally went to your classes or used your services, would they see results?
2. Know some of the things you try won't work. Don't throw the baby out with the bath water; don't assume that if one thing doesn't work, none of it will work. Not all marketing will work for your business, but some of it will, and the only way to know is to try.
3. Leverage multiple marketing channels, swapping out only one at a time after a given channel has had at least four months to show results. If you give up on a channel too early, you'll never know its true potential. If you change multiple channels at once and your results suddenly improve, you may not know which change was responsible.

4. Don't stop when it starts to work. Would you advise your clients to stop working out once they reached their desired weight loss or wellness goals? Of course not. Although newer businesses need to be more aggressive, mature businesses still need to market their services.

5. Be willing to make mistakes, try something new, and do things differently. You must take risks because if you keep doing what you did, you will keep getting what you got.

6. Quantify the results. You cannot tell when your marketing is working if you don't track it.

7. Set SMART (Specific, Measurable, Achievable, Realistic, Timebound) Goals. For more about SMART Goals, go to https://www.indeed .com/career-advice/career-development/smart-goals.

8. Create a simple marketing plan. It's imperative that you have a written marketing plan that you can share with your team so that you have buy-in and everyone knows the plan of action.

9. If you have substantial business goals and a marketing budget of at least a few thousand dollars per month, it may be time to hire a public relations firm. There will always be a need for your business to be reaching out to your local media outlets to let them know when your business has a story to tell worthy of their viewers, readers, or followers. Reach out to local media. Find out what stories they are looking for and let them know that you are happy to be a resource for them.

Steps to Create a Simple Marketing Plan

A **marketing plan** is a document that summarizes your marketing objectives, which media you intend to use to meet those objectives, and a timeline as well as projections of when you expect to see results. The following steps are critical to creating an effective marketing plan:

1. If you currently have a business, evaluate your current marketing tactics. What is working and what is not?

2. Identify your customer personas.

3. Choose your initial three to four marketing strategies and the marketing channels you will use.

4. Create a monthly budget and calendar. Download a free copy of an Annual & Monthly Budget spreadsheet and calendar. (See Appendix.)

5. Have fun with it! Marketing is a creative process and your own personal laboratory. You never know which strategy might hit for your business.

6. Quantify your goals based on key performance indicators—revenue, new clients, referral source, online sales, etc.
7. Gather feedback to inform future offerings. Read survey results and customer reviews, and check in with customers regularly to learn what they love about your offerings and what opportunities you have to improve your business offerings.
8. Review your results monthly and reflect on what's working and what's not. Then discuss these insights with your team, adjust your strategy, and try again.

After reading this chapter, how do you feel? If this content energizes you, then great! You will likely be excellent or even outstanding at planning and overseeing the marketing of your business. If it doesn't, and especially if these topics leave you feeling overwhelmed, then you should delegate or outsource this task to someone else. Whatever you do, don't ignore it. Marketing is a huge part of any business's success and utterly essential to create a wellness business that lasts.

20 | Fuel Your Business with Effective Leadership

Every wellness business owner is a leader. Even if you never hire an employee, you are practicing leadership every time you interact with your clients, vendors, and partners. If you are building a team, then your leadership will make a defining difference. Effective leadership does not require a certain personality type. Instead, effective leadership requires that you know yourself, get yourself out of the way, practice servant leadership, and love people.

Knowing Yourself

What do you stand for? What do you want your life to be about? What are your strengths and weaknesses? What was your childhood like and how does that affect who you are today? What do you want people to say about you after you are gone?

These are deep and important questions for every human being, and we are the only ones who can answer them. In truth, this journey of self-discovery does not end until we do. But the best leaders at some point in their journey reach a threshold of self-awareness that enables them to transcend ego and get themselves out of way. That is when the real breakthrough of effective leadership happens.

Getting Yourself Out of the Way

Effective leadership isn't about you. It's about them—the people you are leading. It's about leveraging your authentic enthusiasm and grit to attract the right people to your team and then applying agile thinking, effective decision making, and adaptability to enable their best performance. It's about creating something bigger than yourself. This can only happen when we get outside of our own heads so that we can be truly conscious of the people we are leading. That is the essence of getting yourself out of the way.

As I think back on the ineffective leaders I encountered in more than three decades of leading and being led by others, in every case their biggest pitfall was not a lack of knowledge or experience. It was their inability to get outside of their own heads. Their attention was clouded by the pain they had suffered in childhood, the resentment they felt toward people who had wronged them, or their own insecurities. They were too inwardly focused to truly see and practice empathy for the people they were responsible for leading.

Think back in your life to someone who had an exceptional impact on your development as a productive adult—perhaps a teacher, director, coach, mentor, or your parents if you're lucky. Do you have them pictured in your mind's eye? Now think of an archetypal moment with them—an interaction that represents their impact on your life. In that moment they are saying something to you that will change your perspective for the better, giving you an insight that will improve your performance and your approach to life. They may even be critiquing or correcting you, and in that moment it may not have felt good to you. But looking back, you realize that their feedback was pivotal for you. Do you have that moment pictured?

Okay, now shift the camera and become that person practicing effective leadership with you. What is going on in their heads in that moment? It's not about them is it? It's about you. They are outside of their own heads and focused completely on you. They have taken the time to truly see you and to understand what you need to be your best self in that moment. They know what you need to hear to learn a valuable life lesson and they are prepared to deliver it. That is that power of getting yourself out of the way and it is the essence of effective leadership.

Practice Servant Leadership

Leaders are called to serve, not to be served. Leaders exist only because there are teams of people who need to be led. While there are some models for self-directed work teams, in most cases a team without an effective leader will flounder like a sports team without a coach.

Therefore, effective leaders must serve their team. To be an effective leader, you must pay attention to every individual, noting the energy they are bringing into your business each day and the quality of the work they are producing; picking up the subtle and not so subtle clues that they are happy or unhappy with their work; and getting closer to team members when you least feel like doing so, such as when their performance is declining or there is suddenly tension between them and you or someone else on the team. Remember that it's not about you, it's about them. It's about what each member of your team needs to deliver their business performance and deliver delightful, habit-forming experiences to your clients.

Effective leadership is also about taking action to remove people who just aren't a good fit. As the boss, this is your most important and difficult responsibility. If you've never managed others before, you might imagine that firing somebody will be easy. It is not. Even if that person's performance is obviously unacceptable; even if they have become like a virus infecting others with negativity and drama, firing people is hard. But you must do it.

Early in the Mindbody story, I was asked to speak on a panel of entrepreneurs in front of a room full of graduate business students. We were the business veterans, and the eager young faces in the audience were there to learn from us. At that point, I was in my mid-30s and had been in Navy and business leadership roles for more than fifteen years. But I had been the CEO of Mindbody for only a short time. One student asked, "What's the most important lesson you have learned as an entrepreneur." I can't even remember my answer, but I remember the answer of the guy sitting next to me, a rather brash Silicon Valley entrepreneur who was leading his second tech startup. He said, "You can't fire people fast enough!"

There was a audible gasp in the room as the student absorbed his answer. I have to admit, he shocked and offended me too. What a terrible thing to say! But I soon learned the wisdom of his words. The basic truth he went on to explain is that by the time we recognize that an employee isn't working out, it is long past the time to let them go. He concluded his insight by saying, "I've never fired somebody and then a week later said, 'I wish they were still here.'" This is because the message to fire someone is coming from our gut, the house of our subconscious where thousands of inputs are recorded by all five of our senses and instantly compared to the lifetime of wisdom we have accumulated.

Meanwhile, our hearts are programmed to avoid pain, including the pain of breaking up with someone, and firing somebody is the ultimate breakup in business. In addition, as entrepreneurs we have a lot on our minds, and our heads are *really* slow at processing everything. Therefore, by the time our head is considering letting somebody go, it is long past the time to do so.

The same dynamic plays out before the firing decision, when we don't proactively address performance issues with our team members. Constructively confronting someone in private when their performance isn't meeting our expectations is hard to do for all the same reasons, and it is an essential element of effective leadership. An outstanding book that will help you understand and manage all of this is *Radical Candor*, by Kim Scott. I highly recommend reading or listening to it before you hire your first employee.

The ultimate truth is that giving candid and constructive feedback to someone we are responsible for, and if necessary, removing them from the team is an act of love. You are loving your team, your business, yourself, and the person you are correcting or letting go. They may learn an important life lesson and go on to great success in some other endeavor. Or they may simply be a better fit on someone else's team. Once you give this candid feedback, you may find that your team feels a closer connection to you because they see that you are willing to be honest and that you have their best interests at heart. And they will see that your heart was really in it with them.

Love People

Good leadership is hard work and it requires an enormous amount of energy. I don't know how to maintain that energy without fundamentally loving the people I work with. Loving people doesn't mean we like everyone. It means that we accept them as human beings. It's the essence of the Hindi greeting shared at the end of every yoga class:

Namaste. The light in me sees the light in you.

There are people we need on our teams that we wouldn't otherwise spend time with. But we can love them for their strengths, weaknesses, and idiosyncrasies. We can love them we they exceed our expectations and when they let us down. And we can love them when we see them put their hearts and souls into our business doing their best to accomplish our mission, even when we fail—especially then. During the many challenging moments at Mindbody, watching our team commit to overnights and work tireless days brought us together like a family.

The challenges that a team faces together can form the foundation for deep love and respect, which are the strengths that your next aspirations can be built upon. This is perhaps the most rewarding aspect of effective leadership.

PART VI | Keep Your Cup Full

21

Staying Well as a Wellness Entrepreneur

The Wellness Entrepreneur's Paradox

Starting and running one's own business is like raising a child. Our heart and soul, hopes and dreams are interwoven with theirs. We feel great when they're flourishing, worried when they're challenged, and devastated when they're not thriving. Regardless of how we feel about them on any given day, our impulse to care for them is never-ending.

As wellness entrepreneurs, this combination of intense emotional involvement and perpetual responsibility can become overwhelming. If we are not mindful of this, our business may begin to degrade our well-being and impact our most important relationships.

In the early years of Mindbody, Blake's and my pace was beyond intense. My job was to run the customer-facing side of the business and his was to develop the product. If I wasn't working twelve-hour days in my garage, I was on the road calling on customers or attending trade shows. Most of the time I loved it. Creating a business from scratch felt exhilarating and it gave me a sense of purpose I'd not felt since the Navy.

In addition, I truly loved our customers, the vast majority of whom are truly wonderful people. Their sense of purpose and humble determination mirrored my own, and their authenticity reminded me of my family. I was working 60+ hours per week and loving every minute of it.

Reflecting back, I realize now that it wasn't the pace of work that degraded my wellness. In fact, taking inspiration from Mindbody's customers, I was exercising more, doing yoga, and eating better. In the first year of Mindbody, I can truly say that our startup had improved my wellness in all seven dimensions. That would soon change.

After the first year my intense focus on Mindbody began to negatively impact other aspects of my life. I began spending less time with my wife, missing some of our kids' events, and letting other important relationships diminish. I justified those sacrifices at the time as necessary. After years of searching I had finally found work I truly loved and had risked our family's financial security to co-found a software company around it. Launching in the wake of the Dot-Com bust we could not attract investors, so I had financed the business with a second mortgage on our home. And there was no financial safety net in our network of family and friends. Failure was simply not an option, there was no financial safety net from our family and friends. The most important thing I could do for my wife and kids was to secure our family's financial future.

Blake's and my partnership, which had started off so beautifully, soon became strained as well. The mountain biking, road trips, and meaningful conversations that used to form the foundation of our friendship soon devolved into terse exchanges about upset customers, product problems, and employee issues. I didn't take the time to notice that Blake was growing increasingly unhappy. For three years prior to accepting me as his business partner, Blake developed the original vision for the company, labored to build our first product around that vision, and onboarded our first twenty customers. When I came with a newcomer's eyes and a deep determination to succeed at all cost, I quickly transformed Blake's creative endeavor into a seemingly endless grind.

As we finished our first year in business, both Blake and I faced a sobering reality that success would be much harder than either of us ever imagined. But we didn't talk about it. We just kept grinding. As one of

Blake's closest friends and his business partner, I was too busy trying to tamp down my own fears and running hard that I didn't take the time to appreciate how he felt from his perspective.

I also wasn't checking in with my wife Lori, who was actually providing the lion's share of our household income, working as many shifts as possible as a labor and delivery nurse. Then 9/11 hit. Our children were 8, 6, and 2.

It took several more years, a broken relationship with Blake, and a divorce from Lori before I truly came to terms with the irony. We had co-founded a business devoted to the wellness industry and we had sacrificed much of our own wellness in the process.

Through the years I have spoken with countless founders and heard similar stories. If you are more than a year into your own entrepreneurial journey, this story may have a familiar ring to you as well. You may face the wellness entrepreneur's paradox: To achieve the success we dream of, our business will inevitably require us to pour our heart into it. And that devotion can easily turn into a form of self-sacrifice that degrades the very principles of wellness that inspired us in the first place.

What to do? I have spent the better part of twenty years wrestling with this wellness entrepreneur's paradox, and I believe the answer lies in the metaphor of *keeping your cup full*.

What Does It Mean to Keep Your Cup Full?

Keeping your cup full is an apt metaphor because it suggests a balance between how much we take from the cup that represents our spirit and energy and how much we put back into it. As a wellness professional, your role is to help fill other people's cups, and most professional coaches and self-help books would focus this entire chapter on the obvious cup-filling activities—exercise, mindfulness, eating right, getting enough sleep, scheduling time for important relationships, and staying connected to your spiritual practice.

Yes, these wellness practices are all important and we actively strive to do all of them. But these alone are not sufficient to keep your cup full if your business is dragging you down. You can't fill a cup that is full of holes. And if your business is overturning your cup on a daily basis, it and you will soon break.

What creates holes in people's cups and ultimately makes wellness difficult or impossible to achieve in their lives? When people fall out of love with their business and when their activities are not focused around their unique ability.

Staying in Love with Your Business

You've got to find what you love.

— *Steve Jobs*

Steve Jobs made this powerful statement in his iconic commencement address at Stanford University in 2005. In fact, in that short and beautifully constructed speech, he used the word *love* ten times. If you have not listened to this speech, or have not done so for a long time, please set this book aside for 15 minutes and go do so now. On your phone or laptop, simply search "Steve Jobs Stanford Commencement Speech" on Google or YouTube.

Okay, are you back? Did that speech touch you? Perhaps even bring a tear to your eye?

Steve Jobs's Stanford commencement address is one of my personal favorites in recent history. I am touched by it every time I listen to it because it is so beautifully crafted and imparts such hard-won wisdom. And I often find myself getting emotional listening to it because we all know the rest of the story.

When he gave this commencement address, Steve Jobs believed that he had beaten pancreatic cancer. But, of course, he had not. His cancer returned a few months later and took his life a few years after that. Steve Jobs didn't know it at the time, but he was in many ways writing his own epitaph with that speech.

I never met Steve Jobs, and based upon his authorized biography by Walter Isaacson, he and I probably would not have hit it off. We differ in our principles of life and leadership in multiple ways. Nevertheless, that speech has left a permanent and deep impression on me. I even have this part posted on the wall near my desk:

> "[Y]ou can't connect the dots looking forward; you can only connect them looking backwards. So you have to trust that the dots will somehow connect in your future. You have to trust in something—your gut,

destiny, life, karma. Whatever. This approach has never let me down and it has made all the difference in my life."

What is he really saying? Make the big decisions in your life with your head, your heart, and your gut all actively engaged—and when those three dimensions of your intelligence are in conflict with each other, let your heart lead.

Steve Jobs's focus on the heart is also revealed by how many times he mentions *love*. For example:

> "You've got to find what you love."
> "I was lucky—I found what I loved to do early in life."
> "I'm convinced that the only thing that kept me going was that I loved what I did."
> "[T]he only way to do great work is to love what you do."

This is powerful stuff, and Jobs's emphasis on the importance of doing what you love has been quoted and paraphrased by business leaders ever since. But what his exhortations of love are missing is any explanation of how you stay in love with the activity. It's as if Jobs believed that once you fall in love with any activity or intention, you will naturally remain in that state of love forever. Obviously, that's ridiculous. People fall out of love with people, activities, and businesses all the time.

In fact, the single biggest determinant of how long any business will last is how long its founder or founders remain passionate and energized by it. And the secret to remaining passionate and energized by your business—to remaining in love with it—is to focus your activities within that business on those things that fuel your passion and energy. That's how you stay in love with what you're doing. And the secret to doing that lies in the principle of *unique ability*.

Identifying and Focusing on Your Unique Ability

Your success will depend in part on the unique ability that you bring to your wellness business. Your unique ability activities will fuel your success. They are the activities that are invaluable to your business and that you love doing.

This is for the simple reason that when you love doing something, you tend to give that activity your full time and attention. The following exercise will help you identify your unique ability as well as identify activities that can be outsourced to others.

Pull out your work calendar and review the past 30 days. Consider each activity you participated in for a moment, and group each into one of these four areas:

1. **Unique Ability Activities.** These activities brought me joy, boosted my energy, and created value for my team and me.

   _____
   _____
   _____
   _____

2. **Excellent Activities.** These activities created important value for my team and me, but they were joy- and energy-neutral—meaning they neither depleted nor fueled my joy and energy.

   _____
   _____
   _____
   _____

3. **Competent Activities.** I completed these tasks adequately, but they diminished my joy and sucked my energy.

   _____
   _____
   _____
   _____

4. **Incompetent Activities.** I did not successfully complete these activities.

   _____
   _____
   _____
   _____

Now review the activities you listed above and consolidate them into the top three or four activities that typify each list. Then record those activities in the four quadrants of the Unique Ability Matrix below.

I hope that your first time doing this exercise and filling out this matrix was as enlightening for you as it was for me. I have done this exercise with

UNIQUE ABILITY ACTIVITIES	EXCELLENT ACTIVITIES
1.	1.
2.	2.
3.	3.
4.	4.
I will focus more of my time doing these most important things.	*I will do these important things until I can easily delegate them to others.*
COMPETENT ACTIVITIES	INCOMPETENT ACTIVITIES
1.	1.
2.	2.
3.	3.
4.	4.
I will delegate or outsource these joy killers as soon as possible.	*I will stop doing these things immediately.*

Figure 21.1   Unique Ability Matrix.

scores of CEOs, business executives, and entrepreneurs, and in every case, the items they listed as unique ability activities were the exact things the world and their organization need them to do more of. The competent activities were ones that could easily be outsourced or delegated to others. Here's the key insight: What is merely a competent activity for you is undoubtably someone else's unique ability activity.

When you have conceived your wellness business properly and designed your own role well, your unique ability activities will be those that are very valuable to your business. If you are like most wellness entrepreneurs, your unique ability activities may include teaching classes or delivering wellness services, leading your team, or building relationships with clients. You may have listed creative activities like developing products or conceiving a marketing campaign. You may have listed financial analysis or business planning. Regardless of what those things are, if they are valuable to your business and you love doing them, those things will fuel the success of your business. This is for the simple reason that when you love doing something, you tend to give that activity your full time and attention. As Steve Jobs said, "[T]he only way to do great work is to love what you do."

So be sure you are focusing the vast majority of your work in your business on your unique ability activities. The more you do so, the more successful you and your business will become.

Your excellent activities are probably essential routines of your business. Since you are really good at doing them and they don't deplete your energy, you will probably need to keep doing most of them for now. As your business grows, however, these will be the activities you gradually hand off to others.

Your competent activities are probably also essential to your business. I can clean our office and balance the books. But if I did that for long, it would drain my energy and make me resentful. Why am I cleaning up after others? If you keep doing these things that drain your energy, you will rapidly fall out of love with your business. Designate someone else to take over these tasks as soon as possible.

If you have anything listed as incompetent activities, you need to ask yourself an important question: Why are you doing these things at all? Whether your incompetent activity is servicing your HVAC system, installing a new toilet, or doing your own taxes, expending your time and energy to do anything in your business that you are lousy at is creating negative value. I am a mediocre house painter. If I picked up a brush or roller to help paint one of Mindbody's offices, I would only mar a job somebody else would do perfectly, and I would really hate doing it.

If you have a voice inside your head saying, "I need to do this to send the right message to my partner or team" or "I can't afford to pay someone else to do this," please stop. Step back, take a deep breath, and engage your creative mind to figure out how to get somebody else to do it.

When you have fully focused your activities in your business on your unique ability, you will stay in love with your business indefinitely, going to work won't feel like work at all, and your cup will stay naturally full. That plus a commitment to the personal wellness practices that work for you will enable you to achieve optimal health and happiness while building a successful wellness business.

And that is how you build a wellness business that lasts.

And for those of us who are called to help others live healthier, happier lives, there can be no greater success.

This is what I wish for you.

Appendix – Resources for Wellness Professionals and Entrepreneurs

Must-Read Books for Wellness Leaders and Entrepreneurs

1. *7 Habits of Highly Effective People* – Stephen Covey
2. *Start with Why / Leaders Eat Last* – Simon Sinek
3. *Blink* – Malcolm Gladwell
4. *E-Myth* – Michael Gerber
5. *Good to Great / Great by Choice* – Jim Collins
6. *Radical Candor* – Kim Scott

Inspirational Short Videos

1. *Stanford Commencement Address* – Steve Jobs (2005)
2. *Grit* – Angela Lee Duckworth (TedGlobal)
3. *Drive: The Surprising Truth About What Motivates Us* – Daniel Pink (with RSA Animate)

Licensing and Certification Programs

Acupuncture

Aspiring acupuncturists must graduate from an accredited school of acupuncture with a master's degree in acupuncture or acupuncture and Oriental medicine. Each state has different licensing requirements and programs vary at each school, but generally training programs range from three to four years, including an internship.

http://acaom.org/directory-menu/directory/

Esthetics

In all states (except Connecticut), estheticians are required to pass an examination and become licensed through their state's board of cosmetology or health department to demonstrate they have received the proper training. Training can be completed at accredited beauty and cosmetology schools.

Massage

Each state has different licensing criteria and requires a minimum number of training hours to obtain a massage therapy license. You may find training through a college, community college, or state-approved school.

American Massage Therapy Association

https://www.amtamassage.org/career_guidance/detail/133?typeId=1

Personal Training and Group Fitness

Prospective trainers can select a specialization that matches their skill sets and professional goals. Do you want to instruct bootcamp-style group fitness? Individualized personal training? Once you determine your path, review the various fitness certifying programs and each of their fitness certifications. Most licensing programs first require that you obtain CPR and AED certifications: https://www.redcross.org/take-a-class/cpr/cpr-training/cpr-certification.

ACE Fitness
> https://www.acefitness.org/fitness-certifications/group-fitness-certification/default.aspx

American College of Sports Medicine (ACSM)
> https://www.acsm.org/get-stay-certified/get-certified/health-fitness-certifications/personal-trainer

Athletics & Fitness Association of America (AFAA)
> https://www.afaa.com/courses/group-ex

National Association of Sports Medicine (NASM)
> https://www.nasm.org/how-to-become-a-personal-trainer

Indoor Cycling

Cycling studios, or gyms that offer cycling, prefer different types of certification. If you are looking for employment, call first to check their requirements.

Schwinn
> https://corehandf.com/certification/

Spinning
> https://spinning.com/become-an-instructor

Pilates

Mat Certification: A mat certification prepares you to teach group mat classes, which is what you will find in most gyms.

Comprehensive Certification: A comprehensive certification prepares you to teach and train clients using traditional Pilates equipment (reformer, chair, trap table/cadillac, etc.) in addition to mat work.

Body Arts and Science International
> https://www.basipilates.com/education/

Peak Pilates
>   https://peakpilates.com/education/certifications/

Power Pilates
>   https://www.powerpilates.com/

Romana's Pilates Instructor Training Program (ITP)
>   https://www.romanaspilates.com/itpoverview

Yoga

A Registered Yoga Teacher must complete training with a Registered Yoga School (RYS®) at the 200- or 500-hour level. Training is available in many different styles of yoga, from hatha to vinyasa, so it may make sense to try as many as you can before committing to a course.

CorePower Yoga
>   https://www.corepoweryoga.com/yoga-teacher-training

RYS® Directory
>   https://www.yogaalliance.org/Directory

YogaTree San Francisco
>   https://www.yogatreesf.com/teacher-training/

Glossary of Marketing Terms

A/B Test: An experiment in which you test a number of variations of an ad or campaign to determine which one performs better.

Bounce Rate (Hard): A hard bounce occurs when the message has been permanently rejected either because the email address is invalid or the email address doesn't exist.

Bounce Rate (Soft): A soft bounce is an email that is temporarily undeliverable, usually because of some problem on the recipient's side.

Buyer Personas: Fictional representations of your ideal customers based on your market research and real data about your existing customers.

Call to Action (CTA): One specific action you want your customer to take when engaging with your marketing (typically buying or learning more in preparation for buying). In sales, it's called asking for the sale. But for you it may mean that you want the customer to click on your website to buy a membership, click on your ad that advertises your discounted package, or book the appointment through your Facebook page. Focusing new prospective customers' attention on the CTA that is most likely to build your business will be your biggest challenge. There are tools that Mindbody offers that can help you with this.

CPC (Cost per Click): Advertising that is paid for only when a customer clicks on your ad.

CPM (Cost per Impression): The rate you pay when your ad is shown per one thousand impressions.

CTR (Click-Through Rate): The number of clicks that your ad receives divided by the number of impressions it receives.

Facebook Page: Facebook pages are for businesses, brands, organizations, and public figures to share their stories and connect with people.

Facebook Profile: A profile is a place on Facebook where you can share information about yourself, such as your interests, photos, videos, current city, and hometown.

Marketing Channels: The means by which your services and products are able to be purchased by your consumers.

Organic Search: The results of entering a search term or string of terms in a search engine that displays your business "organically," having no paid advertising associated with the search engine listing.

Paid Search: Advertisements you pay for through search engine marketing so that your advertisements get matched with users actively searching for the products and services you offer.

SEO (Search Engine Optimization): The process of optimizing web page content so that it is easily discoverable by users who are searching for that content.

Social Media: Websites and applications that enable users to create and share content or to participate in social networking.

Unsubscribe Rate: The percentage of subscribers who have chosen to no longer receive your messages. A rate below 0.2 percent typically indicates that you are within the norm and a rate above 0.5 percent means you have some work to do.

Acknowledgments

This book would not have been possible without the thousands of gritty and innovative entrepreneurs the Mindbody Team and I have had the honor of serving. For all of you who have given me my life's work, I am eternally grateful.

In particular, I would like to thank these wellness industry pioneers whose early faith in Blake Beltram, Mindbody, and me gave our nascent garage startup its legs:

Cynthia Graham – Founder, RPM Fitness Studio

Colin Grant – Founder, Pure International

Sat Jivan Sing and Sat Jivan Kaur Khalsa – Co-Founders, Kundalini Yoga East

Donna Rubin and Jen Lobo – Co-Founders, Bode NYC

Farzeneh Noori – Founder, Yoga House Pasadena

Jasmine Tarkeshi – Founder, Laughing Lotus Yoga

Lynn Whitlow – Founder, Funky Door Yoga

Mari Winsor – Founder, Winsor Fitness Pilates

Michael Ziegler – Founder, 7th Heaven Yoga Berkeley

I would also like to thank these innovative founders whose unique perspectives and heroic stories helped to shape this book:

Alexandra Bonetti Perez – Founder, Bari Studios and TalentHack

Anna Hutz – Founder, Namaste Fitness

Chesley Long – Founder, Camp Yoga

David Long – CEO, Orangetheory Fitness

Joanne Matthews – Founder, Ten Health & Fitness

Sharmila Mitra – Founder, Core Arts Pilates
Ariel Shannon – Founder, Bluebird Salon
Jill Simpson – Founder, Ebb & Flow Yoga
Patti Stark – Founder, Serenity on the Square
Darik Stollmeyer – Founder, Rev SLO
Josh York – Founder, GymGuyz

Through these amazing people—and thousands more like them—I experienced the purpose-driven, entrepreneurial spirit that fuels the wellness industry and learned what it takes to build a business that lasts.

I also want to thank the following individuals:

Blake Beltram, who taught me about boutique wellness twenty-five years ago and brought me into his entrepreneurial vision

Lori Stollmeyer Ryan, who supported my dream of starting Mindbody and worked extra shifts as a labor and delivery nurse to support our family while Mindbody was in our garage

Stender Sweeney, our original angel investor and mentor, who believed in me when no rational investor should have

Bob Murphy, whose investment and talent enabled our journey from tiny startup to publicly traded company

Nadia Adam and Tracy Richmond, who organized the book writing process and kept me on task

Richard Narramore and the Wiley Team, who pulled it all together

All Mindbodyians – past present and future – whose dedication and talent are connecting the world to wellness.

Lastly, I want to thank my wife Jill, whose hero's journey inspired me to write this book, and whose love sustained me while I wrote it.

About the Author

RICK STOLLMEYER co-founded Mindbody in his garage in 2000 and served as the company's CEO until August 2020. During his two-decade tenure as the company's principal leader and visionary, Rick and his co-founders played a key role in the development of the wellness industry—from the introduction of the industry's first integrated online booking and business management capabilities in the early 2000s, to the release of the first fully cloud-based wellness business management solution in 2005, to the groundbreaking Mindbody Consumer App that is used by millions of people today.

Under Rick's leadership, Mindbody became a notable technology platform as well, inspiring hundreds of other tech entrepreneurs to leverage the company's open APIs to build transformational startups of their own. Together, Mindbody and its platform partners have helped to fuel twenty years of massive wellness industry growth.

Today, Mindbody is the leading software platform for the global wellness industry. The company's technology powers tens of thousands of wellness businesses, while its Certified Consultants and Mindbody University educational events help wellness entrepreneurs build wellness businesses that last.

Rick remains closely involved with Mindbody, serving as the company's executive chairman and advocating for entrepreneurialism and the global wellness industry. Rick lives with his wife, Jill, near the company's headquarters in San Luis Obispo, California.

Index

real time tracking/reporting, as a
key payments platform
requirement, 152
Red Cross, 218–219
reengagement offers, as
discounting, 111
referrals
for accountants, 92
for lawyers, 91
Registered Yoga School (RYS),
220
Reiki, emergence of, 30
reports, as a key software platform
requirement, 151
Reserve (Google), 35
resources
books, 217
certification programs,
218–220
inspirational short videos, 217
licensing programs,
218–220
retail options, compared with
home-based and virtual
options, 101–106
retail wellness delivery (Class IV),
101–103
Rev SLO, 66
revenue
about, 69–70
cost of, 70
reward chemical, 114–115
Rockefeller, J. D., 49
role, designing your,
137–145
Romana's Pilates Instructor
Training Program (ITP), 220

Rush Cycle, 34
RYS (Registered Yoga School),
220
RYS Directory, 220

safety, in Maslow's Hierarchy of
Needs, 21–24
sales, cost of, 70
SBA (Small Business
Administration), 187
SBA Guaranteed Loan, 187
Schultz, Howard
*Pour Your Heart into It: How
Starbucks Built a Company One
Cup at a Time,* 112
Schulz, Howard, 112–113
Schwinn, 219
search engine listings,
free, 175–176
search engine marketing (SEM),
192–193
search engine optimization (SEO),
174–175, 221
Second Wave of wellness, 30–33
securing financing, 181–189
selecting
accountants, 93
bookkeepers, 93
integrated payment platforms,
147–158
integrated software platforms,
147–158
lawyers, 91
self-actualization, in Maslow's
Hierarchy of Needs, 21–24
SEM (search engine marketing),
192–193